Ferdinand Anton   Ancient Peruvian Textiles

Ferdinand Anton

ANCIENT PERUVIAN TEXTILES

with 302 illustrations, 112 in colour

Thames and Hudson

For Lisa Schirmer, my editor for many years

at VEB E.A. Seemann Verlag,

and Alan R. Sawyer, the archaeologist

who aroused my interest in ancient Peru and to whom

I owe so much in his role as my mentor.

On the endpapers: painted cotton cloth from the South Coast decorated with a flight of waterfowl, *c.* 300–100 BC (see Pl. 37).

NOTE When no other source is given, the drawings reproduced in the text are from photographs by the author of material in private collections. The drawings themselves are by Inge Brux.

Translated from the German *Altindianische Textilkunst aus Peru* by Michael Heron

First published in Great Britain in 1987 by Thames and Hudson Ltd, London

Printed and bound in the German Democratic Republic

Contents

Previous page:

Fig. 1 A bird, from a slit
tapestry. Chimu style,
c. AD 1200–1450.

Fig. 2 The double-headed
snake motif that appears on one
of the oldest of all surviving
textiles, from Huaca Prieta,
c. 2000–1500 BC, was to recur
throughout Peruvian culture.
(After a reconstruction by
Junius B. Bird)

The Language of Textiles

The written history of the gigantic continent of America, which contains nearly a fifth of the world's population, is brief compared with its long, mysterious prehistory. On 12 October 1492, at about 3 o'clock in the morning, three Spanish ships, seeking a western sea-route to India, found their way barred by what turned out to be the offshore islands of an unknown continent. A 'new world' was suddenly revealed to the astonished eyes of Europe. For some time they could not believe it. Christopher Columbus, the discoverer of this unknown land, died in 1506 still believing he had found the continent of Asia. The name 'West Indies' for the islands and 'Indians' for the inhabitants still preserves this mistake.

A year after Columbus died, in 1507, the Italian navigator Amerigo Vespucci published his book *Mondo Nuovo*, in which he established the truth about the new continent. In the same year the German cartographer Martin Waldseemüller, inspired by Amerigo's book, gave it the name 'Ameriga' in his map of the world. America had acquired a name, but the inhabitants remained 'Indians'.

For the many millennia of America before 1492, archaeological excavation is our only source. To reconstruct history from this material has often been very difficult, requiring much patient work and frequently severe hardship. Not only the remains themselves have to be taken into account, but also where they were found, and how they fit into a system of cultural development. In this jigsaw, ancient Peruvian textiles have been among the most significant pieces. Today the great Indian cultures, their socio-political structures and religious beliefs, and above all their art, are well researched; but the great number of Indian peoples, the enormous area over which they were distributed (*Map, p. 234*), the inaccessibility of many regions, the impenetrable rain forests, the impassable mountains and uninhabited deserts, all present great obstacles to any Americanist and do nothing to facilitate an accurate chronology of Pre-Columbian cultures.

In Peru, where most of the oldest Indian textiles have been found, the presence of Palaeo-Indian hunter-gatherers as long as 20,000 to 23,000 years ago has been attested

Fig. 3   A bird of prey with
a stylized snake inside its
body, from Huaca Prieta,
c. 2000–1800 BC – another motif
found in many guises down to
the Inca period. (After a reconstruction by Junius B. Bird)

by archaeological excavations.[1] The earliest textile fragments of which the patterns
could be reconstructed and which tell us something of the ancient Indians' perception
of the world and artistic abilities were found at Huaca Prieta ('Place of the black-
ened stones'). They are more than 4,000 years old (*Figs. 2, 3*). Very few textiles in the
world are as old as this. Fragments of fabric woven over 3,000 years ago during the first
great culture of ancient Peru, known to us as the Chavín culture, have also been preserved, and these give us an idea of how fascinating the expressive power of the textile
patterns of the period must have been. They are dominated by the imaginative representation of the Staff God, a hybrid anthropomorphic feline carrying ceremonial staves in
the form of snakes (*Fig. 4; Pls. 28, 33*).

   The first professional excavations in which ancient Indian textiles were found were
carried out by two Germans, Alfons Stübel and Wilhelm Reiss, on the Central Coast of
Peru. In their book *Das Totenfeld von Ancon* (Berlin 1880–87) mummies wrapped in
sumptuous cloths, together with their grave goods, were illustrated with great accuracy
for the first time, in superb lithographs. Inspired by this work, the first (but very slim)
volume on the subject of Peruvian textiles, by William H. Holmes, appeared in the Unit-
ed States two years later. Holmes had access to a private collection, as well as to a quantity of fabrics which had recently come into the possession of the Bureau of American
Ethnology of the Smithsonian Institution in Washington. Classification at that time
was impossible. Holmes believed that the textiles almost certainly belonged to the Inca
period:[2]

The grade of culture represented by this work would seem to be very high, considering American products
only, but its equivalent in old world culture must be sought in remote ages. This is shown in striking manner when we place the more delicate pieces of Peruvian work beside fabrics taken from the mummies of
ancient Egypt. In quality of fabric, method of construction, color, and style of embellishment, the correspondence is indeed remarkable. The closest analogy, as far as my observation extends, is with some
Egyptian fabrics of the first few centuries of the Christian era.

Fig. 4 The Feline God or Staff God, with ceremonial staves in the form of double-headed snakes; further snakes emerge from the figure's belt and head. This depiction is on a painted cotton cloth from Carhua in the Paracas peninsula (see Pl. 28). Chavín style, c. 1200–700 BC.

At the time, to compare Peruvian fabrics with those of Coptic Egypt was bold and met with little comprehension. Holmes gave up Perù, and turned his attention to Mexico and Central America, where he gained a great reputation for his research. In fact, his interest in Peruvian textiles had been fortuitous. He had found them in showcases and drawers, out of context and remote from their place of origin – the Peruvian desert.

There is nowhere else in America and hardly anywhere in the world where archaeology has had such an opportunity to enter the world of the dead as it has on the Peruvian coast. There the bodies lie on straw mats – children, adolescents, men and women crouch individually or in a group, their skin dried, their hair still with a slight sheen. Spread out in front of them are bowls full of beans, maize and coca leaves; around them are toys, sewing-boxes with threaded needles, looms with cloths already started or with uncompleted pattern bands (*Pl. 10*), the weaver's 'notebook', which obviously served as a model for the commonest figurative and ornamental weaving patterns. *Plate 11* shows a plain weave cotton fabric with a skein of wool, also found in a grave on the Peruvian coast. At the top it still has the warp beam with the warp threads wrapped round it, decorated with feathers. In many respects such a tomb is more like a workshop during a break than an eternal resting-place. The dead are mostly wrapped in several layers of extremely varied fabrics, from cotton cloth to coarsely plaited nets (*Pl. 4*). The finest and most decorative fabrics were concealed at the very core of the mummy bundle. That explains why so many superb textile fragments have survived. In addition to the lavish cult of the dead of the ancient Peruvian Indians, another circumstance favourable to archaeology is the character of the coast. The area is almost rainfree, and the soil has a high saltpetre content. Even such delicate things as featherwork (*Pl. 177*) and openwork gauze (*Pls. 22, 119*) have been amazingly well preserved for centuries.

The father of Peruvian archaeology was Max Uhle, a German scholar, who over decades of systematic and indefatigable excavation drew back the curtains and revealed pre-Inca cultures. He came to Peru in 1896 and, following Reiss and Stübel, began work

on the burial-ground of Ancón. The temple complex of Pachacamac, a famous pilgrim-age site and hence a meeting place of ideas, art styles and talents, was his next site. It was his most extensive excavation and he found large numbers of clay vessels as well as textiles. The great repertoire of motifs and stylistic variations in these finds stimulated archaeologists to set up a 'type register'. At Pachacamac and at later excavations else-where on the coast Uhle frequently came upon 'Tiahuanacoid' pottery in association with fine textiles in the same style. He was the first to recognize the great age of these artefacts and to identify, on the basis of stylistic similarities in the motifs and design, the extent of this cultural horizon (now known as the Middle Horizon), which preceded that of the Inca by several centuries. We also have to thank Max Uhle, who sacrificed everything to his obsession with field archaeology, for the invention of a methodology of ancient Peruvian styles and cultures. He shared with other pioneers of archaeology, however, the bitter experience of finding behind every door that is opened another that is closed – an endless succession of questions to be answered.

The ancient Peruvians never developed a system of writing. This may have intensi-fied their need to express themselves in other ways. Their 'language' was the form of their reliefs, the painting on their ceramics, and especially the patterns on their textiles. To them the images and signs woven into cloths or embroidered and painted on fabrics, the combination of colours and the manner of composition, were hymns and prayers, thanksgivings and laments, the expression of ideas which priests and rulers knew how to arouse and keep alive in the people. Although one can never be really confident in in-terpreting patterns, it does seem true to say that the textile art of the Indian peoples is the key to their faith and powers of imagination. Is it possible for us to understand what this art was seeking to express? Can we decipher these age-old sources of statements, and even draw conclusions about past cultures from them? Do these wonderful textiles, which have come to light again after hundreds and thousands of years, tell us any more than the fact that the Indian weavers before the Spanish conquest were capable of

Fig.5 *What appears to be a weavers' workshop, painted on a vessel from the Moche culture, c.300–500. (After Julio C. Tello)*

Fig.6 *Feline with anthropomorphic features and snakes, and its cub (bottom right), from an embroidered border. Late Paracas, c.300–200 BC.*

producing striking patterns and admirable colour combinations, and mastering an astonishing variety of techniques?

The oldest, the most beautiful, and, from the technical point of view, the most varied examples of ancient Indian textile art are those of Peru. Almost two hundred colours and shades of colour, as well as nearly every weaving technique known to us today, were in common usage. The textiles were produced on very simple constructions, known to us from graves (*Pl.10*) or the pictorial chronicle of the Indian Huaman Poma de Ayala (*Fig.101*). The weaving process is also clearly visible on a painted jar from the Moche culture (*Fig.5*): the painting presented here as if unrolled from the vessel, which dates from the fourth or fifth century AD, when this extremely realistic art had reached its zenith, seems to show a workshop in the service of a high dignitary where women are working at belt looms.

This belt loom (*Fig.p.233*), also known as a back-strap loom, was used for textile production throughout ancient Peru. The warp was stretched between two parallel wooden rods – the 'warp beam' or 'yarn beam' which might be attached to a post, the wall of a house or a tree, and the 'breast beam' which the weaver held in place by a band round her waist. The slightest movement of her body was enough to tighten or slacken the warp. The basic equipment also included a wooden weaving sword and a heddle. For complicated patterns, women worked with several sheds and heddles enabling them to raise additional warps to form the pattern. This simple and easily portable belt loom was an apparatus with unlimited possibilities in the hands of the Indian woman, and nearly all Peruvian textiles were produced on it. (Two much less common types of loom, a vertical and a horizontal, also existed.)

As in the past, the Indians' main item of clothing is still the *unku*, a sleeveless shirt usually of undyed cotton, often embroidered with brilliantly coloured geometric ornaments. A small sculpture from the Moche culture on the north coast (*Pl.7*), dating from some time between *c.* 100 and 600 AD, shows an ordinary man, perhaps a farmer,

Fig.7   The double-headed snake motif on an ornamental border in the Paracas style, c.500–200 BC.

Fig.8   Stylized feline with its young, depicted on the embroidered border of a Paracas burial cloth, or 'manta', c.500–200 BC.

holding this kind of man's shirt with simple ornamentation. The poncho is similar, but not sewed together under the arms. Tailoring as we think of it was hardly known in the Indian world: the poncho and *unku* consist of strips, and the decorative bands were either woven in or sewn between the strips (*Pl.26*).

The technique of the loom held by a band around the back enabled the individual weaver to produce cloths and ornamental bands of a width varying from 2 cm. to about 1 m. That was adequate for making ponchos or the ground of borders on which imaginative embroidery was worked (*Figs.6–8*). But how did the weavers produce much wider cloths, such as those in which the mummies were wrapped, which in the Paracas and Nazca cultures were as much as 2–4 m. wide? Investigators were long puzzled, until the American archaeologist Junius B. Bird saw a wide cloth being woven in Peru. The solution turned out to be very simple: instead of one woman at the loom there were three, sitting side by side and passing the weft from hand to hand.

It is not known where and when in ancient America the belt loom first appeared. The earliest examples of its use are textiles found at Huaca Prieta, which can be dated to *c.* 1800 BC. At almost the same time the regular cultivation of maize is attested on the Central and North Coasts and ceramics, too, made their first appearance. More recent excavations in the region of Valdivia on the south coast of Ecuador contributed the oldest evidence to date (*c.* 2500 BC) of 'genuine' woven fabrics, i.e. textiles produced on the loom. The fabrics themselves, however, have not survived. Only the impression made by them on clay vessels before firing bears witness to their existence.[3]

Naturally there is also a good deal of mediocre material among the finds of woven fabrics and ceramics. Increase in population and the consequent social, economic and political changes led to a kind of mass production. But an astonishing number of these products must rank as works of art because a creative will unmistakably lies behind them. In addition to this most essential criterion for the application of the notion of 'art'[4] in Indian weaving, there is another. The 'artist' could choose the materials and

techniques to be used in realizing his idea. In spite of the strict style characteristic of a specific region, period and society, the craftsman had a certain freedom in the formal fashioning of motifs, the choice of colours and their combination. Compositions as balanced as those exhibited by many woven fabrics cannot have originated 'instinctively'. They needed preparation and sketches. Peruvian weavers had neither paper nor pencil at their disposal. But their experiments, notes and instructions are preserved in pattern bands (*Fig. 12; Pl. 121*). On some of these the outlines of figures are embroidered in advance, while on others there are more than a dozen different motifs in various techniques.

With their works the anonymous 'artists' of ancient Peru did more than create the striking art style of their period: they also contributed to a far-reaching diffusion of their culture's ideology. From the very beginnings of textile art we find the depiction of certain religious ideas and symbols (*Fig. 2*).

The chief site of the Preceramic IV Period (*c.* 2500–1800 BC) is Huaca Prieta. It is uncertain how the non-woven cloths found there were produced: they seem to have been made with the hands alone, mostly by the twining technique (figure-of-eight twining) which gradually developed from the much older techniques of basketwork and mat plaiting with bast or vegetable fibres. The first raw materials for producing thread – more like cord than thread – were spurge and, somewhat later, agave leaves.

It is to Junius B. Bird that we owe most of what we know about the beginnings of textile art in ancient Peru. In the course of his meticulous excavations at Huaca Prieta he paid attention to the smallest fragments and most insignificant objects, and after his field work was completed he spent years examining under the microscope the 9,000 textile fragments recovered during his various campaigns. He discovered more patterns and motifs than anyone had expected,[5] and succeeded in reconstructing the long-faded designs in the laboratory (*Figs. 2, 3*). He found that colour had come from animal and vegetable dyes and other pigments. The contrast between the various natural colours of

the yarn was skilfully exploited, as well as the differences in the structure of the fabric produced by variations in the weft.

The great age, the patterns, and even more the level of sophistication and the clarity and consistency of the style are simply amazing. In the oldest Peruvian textiles we already find the motifs that formed part of the artists' repertory down to the Inca period (1476–1532). These occur in countless variations both on textiles and on other material: the two-headed snake, the bird of prey with outspread wings, crabs and other marine creatures, and even the representation of one animal inside another – a fertility symbol that was to become common later (*Fig. 3*). In these designs naturalism has already been abandoned: the animals are distanced from reality and mythologized by stylization. Huaca Prieta marks not only the beginning of Peruvian art, but also the birth of its mythology. It seems likely that more ancient textiles have been found in Peru than in the whole of the rest of the world.

The cotton plant provided the first really suitable raw material for textile production. It was spun in Peru on the hand spindle. There is evidence of the cultivation of cotton on the coast as early as *c.* 2500 BC,[6] long before the cultivation of food plants such as maize and beans. The coastal inhabitants soon learnt to value cotton nets for fishing. The great esteem in which the cotton plant was held by the ancient Peruvians is demonstrated by the fact that it was chosen as a motif to decorate textiles (*Figs. 9, 10*).

With the diffusion of the Chavín culture in the first millennium BC, another raw material came from the highlands to the coast, the wool of domesticated South American camelids, the llama and the alpaca. The wool of wild vicuñas was predominantly used in the Inca period. Even bats' fur and sometimes human hair itself was spun into yarn, the latter less for practical reasons than because it had a religious significance. For the Peruvian fabrics that we have been able to recover were not those intended for the living: they clothed and enveloped the dead.

Art as an end in itself and for spiritual edification would have been an utterly alien

Figs. 9, 10   The 'Cotton Deity', incorporating features of the Feline God, on painted cotton cloths from Carhua in the Paracas peninsula. Chavín style, c. 1200–700 BC. (After Alan R. Sawyer)

concept to the Indian cultures. The artistic impulse served religious cults; in particular it helped man to come to terms with the inevitability of death – a mainspring of human behaviour and thought, and a motive for artistic creation. Cloths decorated with embroidered motifs have frequently been found folded up on mummies' chests. Clearly, they were supposed to keep the deceased warm in the icy world of the dead. Junius Bird found on examination that one of these *mantas* or burial mantles was 3.43 m. wide and more than 25 m. long. Laid out in a straight line, the warp thread would be 120 m. long. How much time must the living have spent weaving it!

Man sought to accept and transcend death in many different ways. He tried to create works which he believed would help him to survive death and so overcome it. According to the beliefs of the ancient Peruvians, the dead were close to the gods and demons, and were mediators between this world and the next. If the living managed to keep in the good graces of the dead, they might also win (so they thought) the favour of the supernatural powers. The whole populace, not only the rulers, subscribed to this belief. That does not mean that the Peruvians practised a single uniform cult of the dead and that everyone was equal in death. In the course of time increasingly clear-cut gradations emerged, caused by the formation of an élite and the different functions and tasks performed by its members. Whereas in the Chavinoid Paracas and Early Paracas phases it is hard to perceive any noticeable difference in the quality and quantity of grave goods, in later periods the rank, dignity and prestige of the dead can be calculated from their material possessions. But at no time did the common man lose his place in the world of the dead and his mission as mediator between the living and their gods.

The fabrics with their impressive multi-figured representations characterize a people and its history for us better than the chronicles dictated by rulers for their own ends, the biased accounts of the conquerors or the ruins of magnificent buildings now overgrown by the primeval forest or covered by the desert sands. Patterns, symbols and forms once invented as the expression of certain ideas in the scriptless society of ancient Peru

Fig. 11 An ornamental pattern composed of birds, from a brocaded border. Chancay style, c. 1000–1450.

Fig. 12 A tapestry pattern band with rows of motifs commonly used in textile design (a detail of Pl. 121). Chancay style, c. 1000–1450.

retained their form and meaning (the 'language' which was preserved and understood) in the woven works of succeeding generations. This 'language', however, was subject to the law of change. New ideas and inspirations generated by a changing ideology led to a different way of thinking and the artistic realization of these ideas gradually eliminated the old ones. Then a new style was born. Sometimes old and new concepts would exist side by side, or merge to produce an individual 'language' in fabric patterns. This law of the art of primitive peoples can be applied to every kind of artistic expression, whether ceremonial like that of Chavín, realistic like that of the Moche, stylized and symbolic like that of Nazca, abstractly ornamental and 'cubic' like that of Tiahuanaco, or soberly geometric like that of the Inca Empire.

If we want to understand the 'language' of textiles we cannot isolate them from ancient Peruvian art as a whole. Its motifs do not exist in a vacuum, they are not fortuitous, but always closely connected with contemporary religious and magic conceptions. We find the same themes and images in painting and pottery, in relief and sculpture in clay and stone, and in the decoration of works made of gold, bone or shell. The same motifs were carved in wood, incised on rock or fashioned as architectural details. Artistic statements in those materials are often more accessible to us than those of the fabrics; sometimes they are easier to follow than the complicated iconography of the textile patterns, showing connections which enable us to recognize the mythical beings in the fabrics in their many metamorphoses, and giving us clues to the sense and significance of the magic signs and symbols in their sometimes extremely abstract forms. Consequently when describing textile designs I shall sometimes find it helpful to make comparisons with, for instance, stone reliefs.

In order to understand this art and to approach the imaginary world of gods and demons, to comprehend the variety of styles and forms of expression, one must first visualize the country itself. Peru is a land of geographical and climatic contrasts. The coastal strip, extending over twenty degrees of latitude, consists of desert, with the exception

of some thirty river valleys (*Pls. 2, 3*). It would hardly be a viable environment for a large population if the inhabitants had not, more than 3,000 years ago, begun to make the river oases fertile with the aid of remarkable irrigation systems, some of which are still in use today. Behind this coastal strip, which is only 30 to 80 km. wide, tower the Central Andean mountain ranges, with the highest peaks at an altitude of more than 6,000 m. Between the mountain ranges lie relatively isolated valleys and plateaux at heights varying between 2,000 and 3,500 m. (*Pl. 1*). To the east, where Bolivia and Brazil adjoin Peru, the Andes fall steeply down to the tropical forests of the Amazonian basin and form a natural boundary between peoples and cultures.

The great difference in altitude between the coast and the mountains was in fact much less of an impediment to the diffusion of the ancient cultures than the impassable deserts between the river valleys. Local art styles on the coast which remained confined to small areas and preserved their characteristic features for centuries demonstrate this, as do the three highland cultures, Chavín, Tiahuanaco and Inca, which managed to extend their cultural horizon from the Andes throughout Peru. Each of these expansions led to intrusive cultural changes mainly connected with the spread of new religious ideas, and was expressed by a distinctive art style. Between these 'horizons' lay periods without cultural unity with several local art styles and cultures of different character existing simultaneously or overlapping. To the archaeologist, these contrasting currents, clearly recognizable in the style of grave goods, represent something like the annual rings on a tree. They are the basis of the chronology of the whole of ancient Peruvian culture.

The division into 'horizons' and 'intermediate periods', however, should not be looked on as rigid. Different styles often coexisted for long periods – one slowly dying out, while another was winning a footing. Art, carried along on the river of history, reflects the essence of the society that produces it by its different trends and styles. And Peruvian textiles, because of their great variety, are a medium through which the

progress of different cultures, the sudden flaring up of religious impulses, and their decadence, became clearly visible.

By and large Peruvian art can be seen as the product of two opposing tendencies: one representational or realistic, and the other non-representational or abstract. In the Early Horizon, which starts *c.* 1200 BC and comprises the Chavín culture and the Early Paracas phases, it is the tendency towards abstraction which is dominant. Hybrid creatures with both human and animal attributes, primarily feline (the Feline God), embody the basic religious ideas, and the impressive art style contributes to their diffusion throughout most of Peru. In the Early Intermediate Period, representational thought and lively imagination modify this ideology and symbolism and permit a naturalistic tendency to take over. A fondness for ornamental embellishment and a growing preference for depicting the real world pulled the Chavín gods from their throne, robbed them of their magic and often endowed them with an almost mundane, non-supernatural character. Even so, the feline is still central, although generally transformed into ornaments on decorative embroidered borders (*Figs. 6, 8*). Concurrently, felines became increasingly part of the trophy head cult. On the South Coast, in the less fertile river valleys between wide strips of coast where the struggle for existence was particularly hard, an awareness of death was more pervasive than in the highlands. In Nazca culture, as in the Late Paracas period, the feline was seen as the 'bringer of food', and the trophy heads which decorate garments and cloths together with vegetation gods or warriors point to man's duty to offer sacrifices (*Pl. 12*). So we have the development of an art in which, despite the presence of naturalistic elements, over-refined stylization and an ever-increasing complexity of symbolism confront us with many puzzles (*Fig. 14*).

The second half of the first millennium BC saw a revival of deep religious impulses. The art which expressed the ideas of Tiahuanaco and Huari had to explore new paths, without renouncing tradition, and so took an important step further than the Chavín 'artists' could. Henceforth, the degree of abstraction is not governed simply by its

Fig. 15 A curious hybrid creature, often used with slight variations as a motif on slit tapestries from the coast, right up to the time of the Spanish conquest – c. 1300–1530 (cf. Fig. 90 and Pl. 166).

1 Machu Picchu, a hilltop settlement of the Inca period, 1476–1532.

effectiveness in expressing ideas, but seems to have a formal basis. Thus the gods of Tiahuanaco are broken down into basic cube-like forms and turned into geometric ornaments, in which the central figure and supplementary filler details are at first barely recognizable to the inexperienced eye (see *Pl. 79* and *Fig. 68*). With their intellectual character, colour composition and clear linear rhythm, these patterns look as if they were designed on the drawing-board. This stylization is not dictated by the weaving process: if anything it is deliberately introduced to deprive the figures of reality and raise them to a divine level. The all-encompassing abstraction gives the textile images a magical suggestive power and almost seems to anticipate Cubism. The marked religious tendency of the Tiahuanaco and Huari cultures which spread throughout Peru and were dominant in the Middle Horizon (*c.* 600–1000) lost its power in the Late Intermediate Period (*c.* 1000–1476), the age of what the Spanish later called the 'little kingdoms', when the theocracy collapsed. Natural models and realistic imagery now come to the fore and for the first time give scope for comparatively free artistic creation. The painted cotton cloths are eloquent examples of this. Painting in the Chavín period was governed by a strict canon (Chavinoid Paracas phase, *Pl. 28*). In the Late Intermediate Period the 'artist' could also introduce his individual manner of expression when painting fabrics with mythological themes. This entirely different imagery is also found in the charming border motifs produced by various techniques (*Pls. 24, 150–153*). In them an animal world close to nature predominates.

With the rise of the Inca Empire, in the Late Horizon (1476–1532), an entirely new artistic manner appeared, characterized chiefly by a geometry from which stylized figures disappear (*Pl. 182*). This new beginning is clearly recognizable, but the Spanish conquest in 1532 put a stop to its diffusion. The mighty empire lasted for a mere six decades, too brief a period for a new artistic trend to take root in the 'little kingdoms' that were annexed. As a result figurative textile motifs in the ancient tradition lived on along the coast of Peru side by side with the characteristic geometric Inca style.

2

3

2 *Chuquitanta (El Paraíso), an architectural complex of the Preceramic Period, c. 2500–1800 BC.*

3 *The decoration on the buildings of Chanchan is identical to that on many textiles of the same period. Chimu, c. 1000–1450.*

4 *Mummy bundle with a false wooden head and eyes of shell inlay. The body is wrapped in several layers of different cotton cloths and coarsely plaited nets. The fine decorative fabrics are at the core of the bundle, and are thus protected. Pachacamac, c. 1000–1470.*

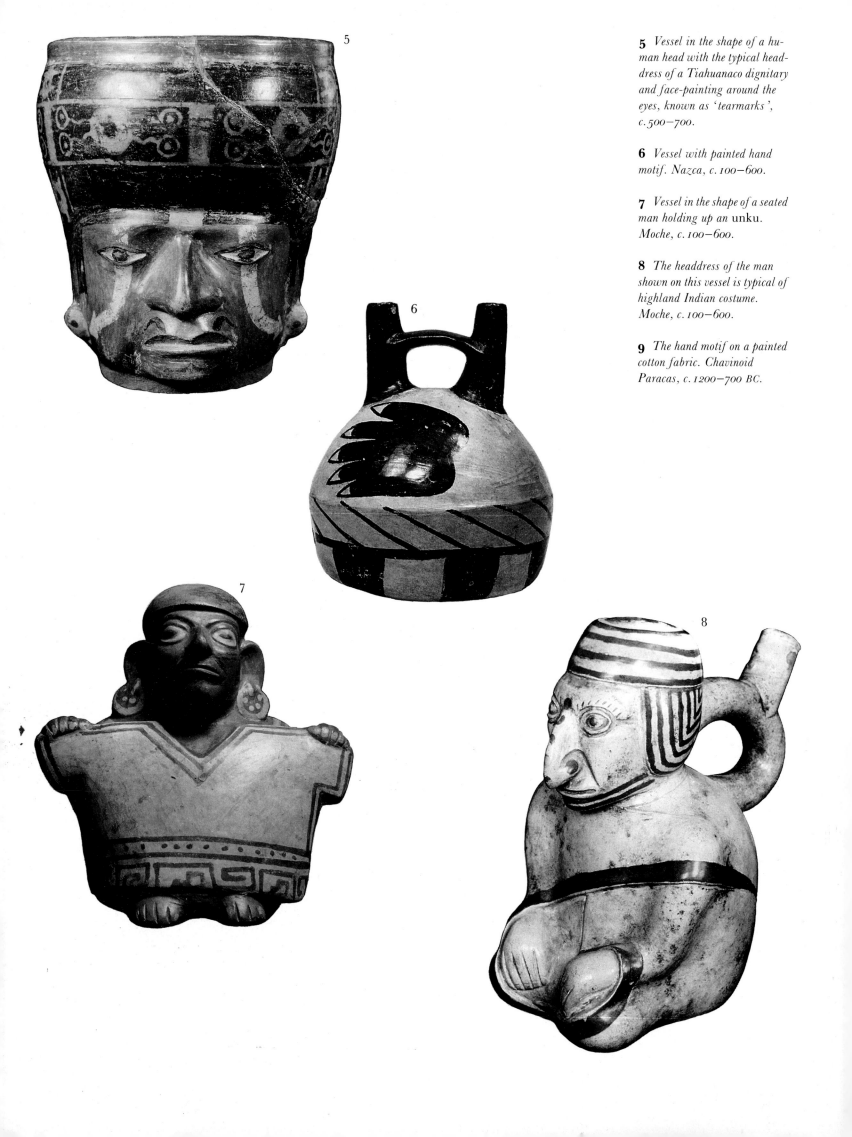

5

6

7

8

5 *Vessel in the shape of a human head with the typical headdress of a Tiahuanaco dignitary and face-painting around the eyes, known as 'tearmarks', c. 500–700.*

6 *Vessel with painted hand motif. Nazca, c. 100–600.*

7 *Vessel in the shape of a seated man holding up an* unku. *Moche, c. 100–600.*

8 *The headdress of the man shown on this vessel is typical of highland Indian costume. Moche, c. 100–600.*

9 *The hand motif on a painted cotton fabric. Chavinoid Paracas, c. 1200–700 BC.*

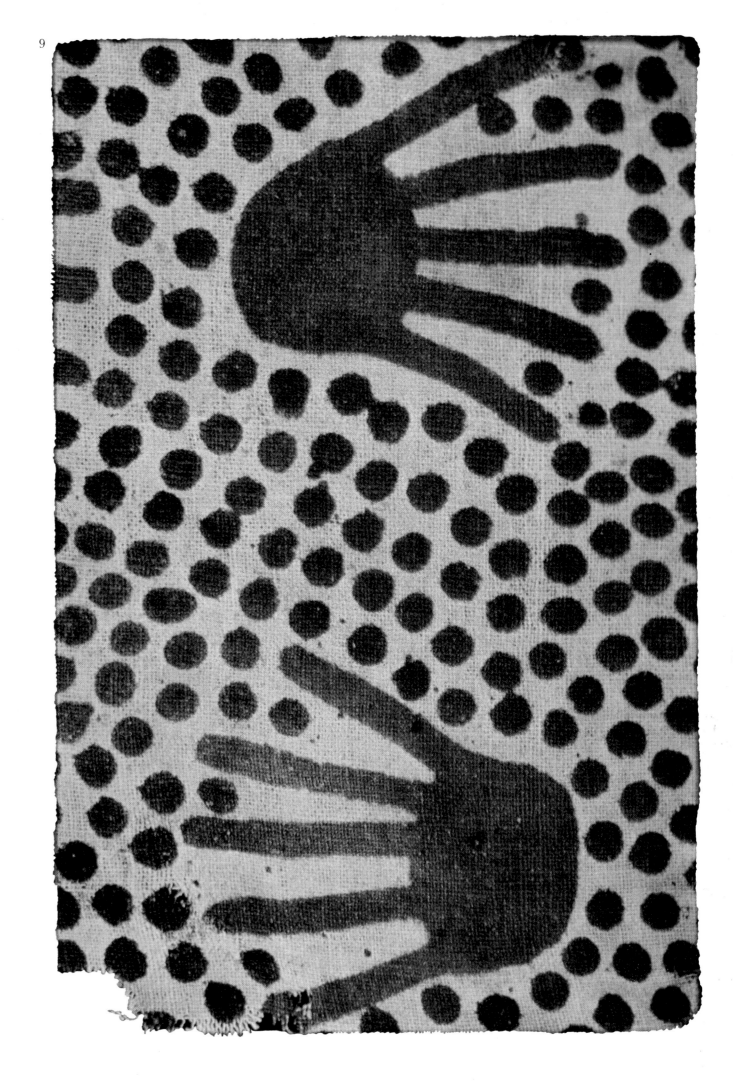

10 *Loom with an unfinished pattern band textile, buried with a weaver to accompany him in the kingdom of the dead. Chancay, c. 1000–1450.*

11 *Another apparently unfinished object associated with the weaver's art. These painted cotton cloths, known as 'mummy masks', were sewn onto the mummy bundle to ward off evil spirits (see Fig. 32). Late Ocucaje phase of the Paracas culture, c. 500 BC.*

10

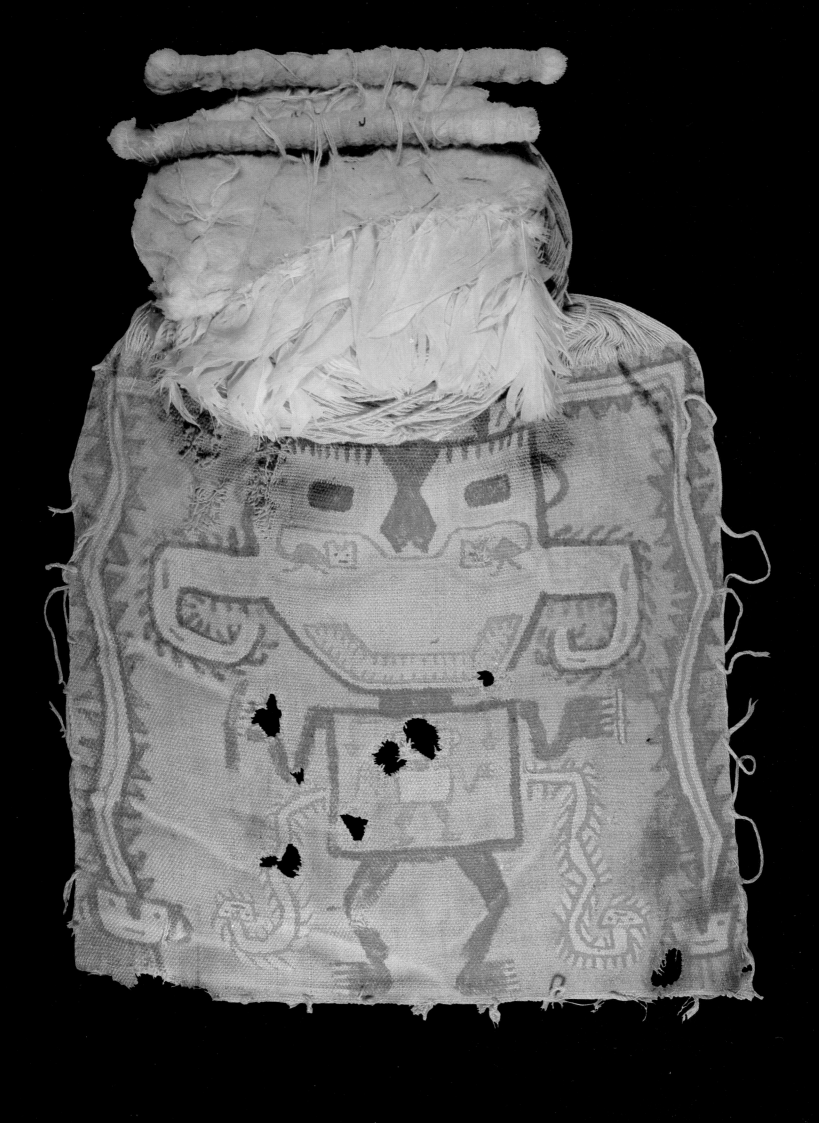

16

17

18

19

20 21

16 *Detail of a decorative border in slit tapestry. Tiahuanaco-Huari style, c. 700–1000.*

17 *Ornamental band with bird motif in wool brocade. Chimu style (?), c. 1000–1460.*

18 *A cotton fabric decorated in the same way. Central or North Coast, c. 1000–1460.*

19 *Coca bag of tapestry with brocaded side border. Tiahuanaco-Huari style, c. 700–1000.*

20, 21 *Front and back of a brocaded plain weave cloth. Chimu (?), c. 1000–1450.*

22 *Openwork gauze with a pattern of stylized cats and birds. Chancay style, c. 1000–1400.*

22

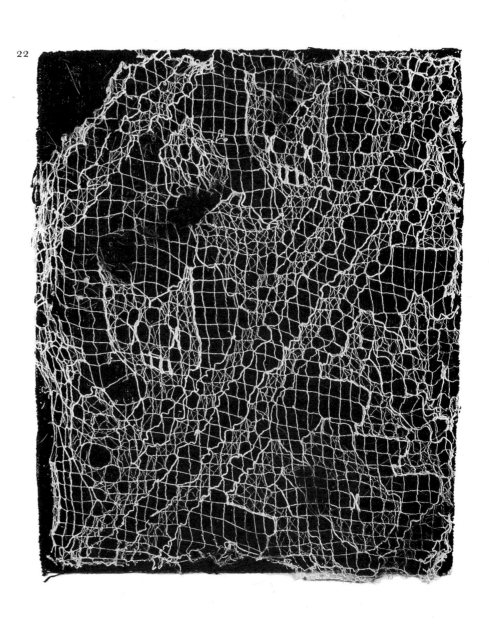

23

24

26 *Garment in plain weave, decorated with fringe, slit tapestry borders, and brocade-work threads. Probably South Coast, Late Intermediate Period or Late Horizon, c. 1000–1500.*

The Divine Image in the Chavín Culture

The initial phase of the Chavín culture, some 3,000 years ago, was a decisive moment in the history of the Peruvian people. It was then that the Northern Highlands developed a divine image so impressive that it was to dominate both religion and art for a very long time, and from there that an art style of extremely high quality spread throughout most of the area of present-day Peru. The culture takes its name from the village of Chavín de Huántar, which lies at an altitude of 3,177 m. and is the site of one of the most important ceremonial centres in ancient Peruvian culture. The complex at Chavín is not particularly large: several buildings erected on platforms are sited around rectangular assembly spaces and a courtyard in an area of little more than 200 square metres.

The decoration of the buildings is remarkable. Sculptures in the round of mythical animals and hybrid creatures are tenoned to the façade of the main temple (*Pl. 27*), and there are reliefs, columns (mostly decorated with incised work), and other architectural elements depicting the Chavín deities (*Pls. 29, 32*). These brilliant designs recur as decorative motifs on the ceramics and textiles of the period (*Figs. 16–18; Pls. 28, 30*), displaying both the mythology and the intriguing art style of Chavín. The feline, specifically the jaguar, is dominant, but snakes, alligators and birds of prey also appear both in realistic and in highly stylized form, as monsters which often have human attributes. The iconography of this art is well thought out, its style accomplished. It expresses a powerful nature-religion which seems intended to arouse both fear and hope.

Unfortunately only a few fragments of textiles which can be directly associated with the Chavín Highland culture have been found on the North Coast.[7] Some of them exhibit the earliest use of new techniques. We find cotton fabrics with supplementary weft, as well as woven materials with discontinuous weft, as opposed to the older fabrics, which were produced solely with a continuous weft. Further south excavations have been more productive, especially in the centre of the South Coast. The finds from this region, mainly the result of grave robberies, are the only representative specimens of genuine Early Horizon textile art in which painted plain weave cotton fabrics mark

*Fig. 16   The Chavín Feline
God as Staff God, with its
essential attributes — fangs,
talons of a bird of prey, and
ceremonial staves — on a painted
cotton cloth from Callango on
the South Coast. (After
Alan R. Sawyer)*

Figs. 17, 18 Two vessels with incised ornament depicting the Feline God of Chavín, with its exaggerated fangs. (Private collection, Buenos Aires)

the beginning of the development of the Chavín style. They represent astonishing early explorations of the possibilities of artistic expression in this material (*Fig. 16; Pls. 28, 30, 33*).

The painting technique is interesting. Paint brushes were unknown to the Chavín artists, and instead they used small sticks with a wad of cotton on the tip. The colours came from both organic and mineral pigments. Their range was limited to red, blue, and shades from ochre to blackish brown for the dark tones. In addition there was the natural colour of the cotton (white to brown) as a ground, which the artist skilfully made use of in the design to achieve contrasts and lend the painting a certain depth.

Not only religious ideas but new materials came from the highlands to the coast. The possibility of employing finely spun wool from South American camelids (alpaca, etc.) and dyeing it in many ways led, for example, to the development and intensive use of covering stem-stitch embroidery in the Middle Paracas period (*c.* 500–300 BC), which facilitated new forms of artistic creation (see eg. *Pl. 43*). Cotton fabrics, still woven in the usual plain weave, were decorated with borders and hems on which embroidery appeared in an inexhaustible wealth of colours and patterns. Whole fabrics were ornamented in this way. The effort and devotion demanded by such work is shown by a burial cloth found on a mummy bundle of the Paracas period, the embroidery of which was composed of no less than 1,200,000 stitches. The use of different yarns and the introduction of wool on an equal footing with long dominant cotton in the Early Horizon opened the way for further developments in weaving and embroidery, culminating in the three-dimensional loop stitch, a technique used only in Peru (*Pls. 31, 38, 56, 57*).

The aim of this introduction to ancient Peruvian textile art, however, is not an enumeration and exposition of techniques or an analysis of colours (of which details are given in the notes on the plates), but the interpretation and classification of textile patterns. We must never forget the close relations that existed between textile art and other spheres of life – economy, society, religion – in these ancient Indian cultures, and it is

therefore necessary to consider these subjects in order to elucidate the meaning of the patterns.

Chavín de Huántar was the religious and intellectual centre of the Early Horizon. It was not the place where the Peruvian gods were 'born' but it was the place where they took form, where art and religion fused into a unity. It is now accepted that the Early Horizon was diffused from Chavín de Huántar until it became the basic culture of the whole of Peru. The Chavín style shows hardly any formative period: it looks more like the flowering of a development whose origins go far back in time.[8] Although one must always reckon with the unexpected in archaeology, it would be a miracle if such a refined art as that of Chavín, in which theocratic ideas were so consummately transformed into images, had evolved overnight. But detailed knowledge of an initial period or early stages of development of this aesthetically and technically mature art style is still lacking.[9]

We do not know how the weavers and embroiderers chose the motifs and colours for their patterns, though it is unlikely that individual taste and artistic feeling were the determinant factors. Markedly different decorative elements are often found on the same site; mythological motifs appear next to patterns taken straight from the natural environment of the coast-dwellers (*Pl. 37*). Yet the majority of textile images refer to the feline in a more or less stylized form. The focal point of religious worship in the Chavín and subsequent cultures was the Feline God, often also known as the Staff God, because it is mostly portrayed carrying a staff or baton (*Fig. 16*). Its fangs and talons, symbols of the deity, are the main theme of this art, characteristics expressing the divine, the supernatural. This feline with anthropomorphic features, which appears on the oldest surviving fabrics (*Pls. 28, 30*), became the ancestor of many Peruvian gods and appears in numerous variations in all pre-Inca cultures (fertility demon or food bringer among the Nazca, jaguar priest among the Mochica). The predator attributes, fangs and talons, exaggerated in the Chavín style, diminish steadily with the passage of time until the

Fig. 19 The Feline God with a body incorporating a stylized snake, from which snakes' heads emerge, as it appears on a stone relief at Chavín de Huántar.

Fig. 20 Feline attributes combined with the body of a bird of prey, from the incised decoration of a Chavín vessel. (Private collection, Buenos Aires)

feline is ultimately prettified into a harmless cat. The Feline God is better fitted than any other motif to guide us through the varied formal language of ancient Peruvian textiles.

The artists' task in this early period seems to have consisted primarily in expounding and diffusing this religious cult. Their task was to find ways of expressing its ideology so impressively, intelligibly and convincingly that the great majority of people could accept it. Artists are spokesmen for the community, expressing the ideas and perceptions of their time and their society in their works. The artist of the Chavín culture subordinated the real world to a conceptual world. He followed no real model, but combined many creatures (predatory feline, man, bird, fish, snake, etc.) into supernatural divine beings (*Figs. 19–26*). The characteristics of jaguar or puma, condor, eagle or falcon are familiar to every Peruvian. The fascination exercised by snakes is something we ourselves can feel. By depicting admired or feared animals or even their characteristic features (fangs, talons, nostrils, wings), the artist directly addresses the senses and arouses certain specific associations in the beholder. His art is essentially directed to the spirit, but sensuous perception of the motif facilitates access to it.

By the time of the Chavín culture, the Feline God was already the most important deity in the ancient Peruvian pantheon. There is hardly a better example of this, both ideologically and formally, than the Raimondi Stele. This monolith, some 2 m. high, is named after the Italian Antonio Raimondi, who discovered it at Chavín de Huántar in the middle of the last century and deposited it in the Lima Museum. All the essential religious ideas which animated later generations in ancient Peru are already expressed in its low relief. It is a masterpiece of Indian art, which compellingly demonstrates the distinctive features of Indian aesthetic and religious concepts. Its complicated elements, which constantly recur in many metamorphoses as textile patterns, are most clearly seen in a drawing (*Fig. 21* and *bookmark*). If you slowly turn the drawing upsidedown and look at the details from every direction, you will discover several faces of the

41

Fig. 21 A schematic representation of the image on the Raimondi Stele, from Chavín de Huántar. The figure and its headdress display the attributes of the feline, the bird of prey, and the snake, the primeval fertility symbol. This drawing is also reproduced on a separate bookmark. If you turn that upside-down and place it next to this illustration, a number of hidden images appear, in a way that is characteristic of ancient Indian art; the eyes, the fangs, the talons and the serpents reappear, seen in a different perspective.

Fig. 22 The pattern on a painted fabric in Chavín style from Callango has the same quality as that of the carved Raimondi Stele (Fig. 21): when the image is viewed from the side or upside-down a wealth of further details, all based on the Feline God, is disclosed. (After John Howland Rowe)

43

Fig. 23   The Feline God with characteristics of condor and jaguar, on a stone relief at Chavín de Huántar.

Figs. 24–26   The Feline God as hybrid creature: two patterns incised on ceramics (top, in a private collection in Buenos Aires; centre, in the Brooklyn Museum, New York), and one painted on a cotton cloth (bottom: see Pl. 33).

Feline God in a single figure. This denotes extremely careful planning. Nothing is left to chance in Chavín art. Even the smallest details of the ceremonial staves which the feline holds in its claws have symbolic importance and contribute to the magic it radiates. The extremely large headdress is unusual. Substantially higher than the whole anthropomorphic body of the god, it consists of several superimposed mythical animals' heads, with naturalistic and stylized snakes emerging from them. The individual details vary slightly, but the basic structure remains. Hence the motifs fit 'seamlessly' into each other and create the impression of a single being, yet at the same time the combination is so skilful that it multiplies the demonic faces concealed in the headdress and increases the variety of their expression. The essential feature, both in the whole design and in the details, is the eyes. Through them the mythical being is made real. The way in which the stylization is done reveals new aspects with every change in the spectator's viewpoint. The tremendous power of *mimesis*, which first strikes us when we look at it from different directions, is one of the main sources of the magic that emanates from the divine figure.

The representation of the god is no less powerful when transferred to other materials, such as clay or cloth. If we look similarly from all directions at the ambiguous feline head on a textile (*Fig. 22*) it becomes clear that an attempt has been made to depict a deity embodying both the 'Lord of the Upper World' and the 'Lord of the Underworld'.[10] The same applies to the reconstruction of a painted cotton fabric in the classical Chavín style, of which the pattern corresponds to that of a Northern Highland stone relief (*Pl. 36*). Here too we have a representation of the central Feline God. Its multiple visages are unmistakable and once again, if we look at the details from different directions, starting with the eyes and fangs, we realize that in Chavín art, as later in the art of Tiahuanaco, nothing is fortuitous.

The religious ideas and art style of Chavín encountered comparatively developed political and social structures in the coastal region, and it is not surprising that local stylistic variations evolved. On the coast, where most food came from the sea, feline

Figs. 27, 28 Hybrid creatures typical of Chavín art, on a vessel from the South Coast (left) and in a now-destroyed mural in the temple of Punkuri. (After Julio C. Tello)

attributes merged with the body of a fish (*Fig. 27*); but the Staff God remains discernible in most of the decoration on coastal textiles and pottery.

Unfortunately nearly all known Early Horizon textiles have come from grave robberies. To sell them more easily and get higher prices, the robbers or *huaqueros* cut their finds up, and threw away the 'worthless' bits. Of the good fragments most went directly into inaccessible private collections. Before 1971 very few painted cotton fabrics with the characteristic Chavín motifs were known, and those were said to have come from Callango in the Ica valley (*Figs. 16, 22; Pl. 28*). Not so long ago a large number of textile fragments, all painted in the same Chavín style, came on to the black market from a site called Carhua, in the south of the Paracas peninsula (*Figs. 4, 9, 10; Pls. 30, 33*), and Alan R. Sawyer, former Director of the Textile Museum in Washington, was able to examine some of them before they were dispersed.[11] It is not known whether they served the cult of the dead or whether, as some researchers suggested, they were wall-hangings in religious buildings.

These textile designs are so similar to the motifs of stone reliefs at Chavín that one is tempted to call them 'copies', and Alan R. Sawyer does not rule out the possibility that they were painted at the cult centre to serve as propaganda: easily transportable, they might have been used to introduce Chavín religious symbolism and its associated art style to the people on the South Coast (see *Pl. 36*). Merchants from the Northern Highlands travelled to the south, perhaps attracted by the high quality cotton found there. The inhabitants of the South Coast were well aware of the source of their wealth. As we have seen, they personified the cotton plant (*Figs. 9, 10*) and gave it divine status.

While the conceptual world of Chavín influenced the inhabitants of the South Coast, their landscape and environment were also woven into their imagery. This produced the Paracas style, to which the next chapter is mainly devoted. The feline remained the dominant figure, but there were significant changes. In the classic Chavín style the feline and its attributes were shown either in profile or full-face (*Pls. 28, 30*). The South

Coast artists, on the other hand, depicted the jaguar or jaguar-hybrid in a mixture of profile and front view (*Fig. 20*). There was a noticeable turn towards realism. The Chavín deities were demoted. The trophy head cult formed the focal point of the new conception of art; in the emergent Paracas style, the severed head of the enemy became the vital symbol of magical powers.

If we look at the Paracas culture in purely chronological terms, all but the Late phase fits neatly into the Early Horizon. But if we decide to include all the other aspects which make up the essence of a culture, the various intellectual currents and stylistic differences in its art begin to pose problems. There is no clear-cut transition to the Early Intermediate period. Some locally conditioned elements exist in similar form in different regions, while some from the same place and the same period show marked differences. Especially with textiles, classification is often dependent on individual factors and so can vary considerably. Some places clung to their traditions for centuries longer than their neighbours, while in others the old coexisted with the new. Thus the transitions from the Chavín style to the subsequent Paracas style and then to Nazca art are so fluid and so varied from region to region that we shall repeatedly have to return in the next chapter to elements which were already formed in the Chavín period, whereas it seems appropriate to examine further developments on the South Coast in more detail here.

The first phase, known as Chavinoid Paracas (*c.* 1200–700 BC), belongs to the Early Horizon. The painted cotton fabrics of this period show unmistakable Chavín elements. Towards the end of the Chavinoid Paracas phase and the beginning of Early Paracas (*c.* 700–500 BC), new weaving techniques and new methods of yarn-dyeing appear, but Chavín influence is still predominant. That is no longer true in the Middle Paracas phase (*c.* 500–300 BC). The unified image disappears and gives way to several regional styles. The production of textiles, which developed a variety of new creative possibilities through new techniques of spinning, dyeing and weaving, increased. Chavín elements

Fig. 29 The Oculate Being, here combined with the features of a crab or spider, on a Paracas embroidered border.

27 A Chavín deity set into the masonry of the main pyramid at Chavín de Huántar, c. 1200–400 BC.

were still used to a large extent, though their purpose and significance seem to have changed. The new god of the so-called Ocucaje tradition is a curiously attractive creature with enormous eyes, smiling mouth and no fangs (*Fig. 29*).

This fertility god, the 'Oculate Being', appears in conjunction with decorative borders on fabrics which, uniquely at Ocucaje between 700 and 500 BC, were loosely stitched to the mummy bundle to act as protective spirits (*Fig. 32*). The god is often depicted standing (*Pls. 11, 41, 42*), with snakes emerging from its head. A similar being (sometimes two) crouches inside its body. A human face may have felines painted on it (*Pl. 40*).

These painted 'mummy masks' are in every respect the strangest products of the Peruvian weavers. In their posture the mythical beings are still remotely reminiscent of the Chavín Staff God. Although in no way comparable to the consummate paintings of the Chavinoid Paracas phase, the childishly drawn god can nevertheless be identified with subsequent representations on fabrics in which the Oculate Being appears as the focal point of much more complicated compositions (*Fig. 36*). This suggests that we should see in the crudely sketched mythical beings the artists' first steps in those new forms of expression which develop fully in the Paracas and the Nazca style.

28

29

28 One of the oldest extant cotton textiles. The Feline God or Staff God already makes its appearance, in profile above and front view below. Chavinoid Paracas, c. 1200–700 BC.

29 Relief slab showing the Feline God in profile, or a priest representing it, much as in the textile above. Chavín, c. 1200–400 BC.

30 A painted cotton cloth depicting the Feline God with its head in profile and its body seen frontally. Chavinoid Paracas, from Carhua, c. 1200–700 BC.

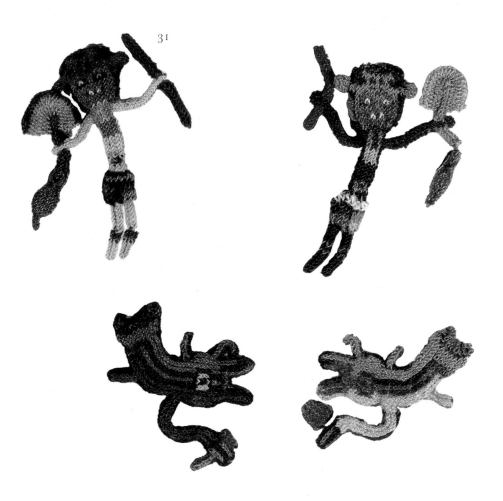

31 *Dancers, warriors or shamans, and fish demons – reminiscent of the motif on a Chavín petroglyph (Pl. 32) – from the border of a burial cloth, embroidered in cross-knit loop stitch. Late Paracas/Proto-Nazca, c. 300–100 BC.*

32 *A petroglyph showing the Chavín god with human, fish and feline attributes. Chavín style, c. 1200–700 BC.*

33 *The feline motif on a painted cloth, incorporating snakes and the beak of the bird of prey (see Fig. 26). Chavinoid Paracas, c. 1200–700 BC.*

34 *Coloured wool embroidery of stylized feline heads seen frontally, on an undyed cotton textile. Probably Early Paracas, early Callango style, c. 700–500 BC.*

35 *The stylized feline head incised on the interior of a bowl. Early Paracas, Callango style, c. 700–500 BC.*

36 *The feline motif in classic Chavín style. This copy of a Northern Highlands stone relief was made to show how such a design might appear on a painted cloth. Such easily transportable objects could then diffuse their makers' style and ideas throughout Peru.*

35

36

37

38

37 *Burial cloth painted with a flight of waterfowl – one of the naturalistic subjects that coexist with mythological and stylized images on Paracas textiles. Late Paracas/Proto-Nazca, c. 300–100 BC.*

38 *Two stylized trophy heads, embroidered in cross-knit loop stitch. Late Paracas/Proto-Nazca, c. 300–100 BC.*

39 *The increasing importance of the trophy head cult is suggested by this detail of an ornamental band in slit tapestry probably from the Late Nazca culture, c. 400–600.*

40

40–42 *Three 'mummy masks', painted cloths sewn to the mummy bundle in the Ocucaje region to serve as protective spirits (see Fig. 32). Paracas, c. 500 BC.*

41

Overleaf:

43 *Detail of an ornamental border incorporating felines and snakes with anthropomorphic features, embroidered in covering stem stitch. Middle Paracas, c. 500–300 BC.*

From Paracas to Nazca

'Paracas' is the name of the wind which blows every afternoon on the coast of southern Peru and northern Chile when the cold air of the sea, which the Humboldt Current brings from the Antarctic ice, meets the hot air above the mainland. The cool breeze which sets both sea and desert in motion does not slacken until after sunset. 'The Paracas is blowing', people say, when the wind roars over the arid desert. In Quechua, the official language of the Incas once spoken throughout Peru, 'Paracas' meant specifically 'sand blown by the wind'. Later it came to signify the wind itself, and later still it was applied as a geographical name to a sandy peninsula stretching into the Pacific Ocean between the fertile valleys of the Pisco to the north and the Ica to the south-east. It is a desolate landscape, like an uninhabited planet. There is no vegetation apart from a few greenish-brown grasses which draw moisture from the air in the shelter of the dunes. Low ranges of hills form sculptured shapes in the vast expanse of sand and animate it with the bizarre shadows they cast.

For archaeologists 'Paracas' is both a pre-Inca culture not simply confined to the peninsula and a particular art style partly attributable to the Early Horizon, partly to the Early Intermediate period. In the mid-1920s the Peruvian archaeologist Julio C. Tello, to whom we owe the terms Paracas culture and Paracas style, discovered sites with extensive burial complexes in many places in the Cerro Colorado on the edge of the Paracas peninsula. He found traces of human settlements – ruins and a little domestic waste – only in the north of the chain of hills, at a site which he christened Cabeza Larga ('Long Head') because of the artificially elongated skulls of the four skeletons he found there.

Two more, very different burial places in the Cerro Colorado were to become highly important for archaeology. The only thing they have in common at first sight is the burial of the dead in a flexed position inside layers of cloth forming a 'bundle'. At one place the dead were in bottle-shaped chambers (*cavernas*) cut deep into the rock of the mountains. Many of these shaft graves reach a depth of 6 m. and some of them have a wall round the top. The special feature of these often very spacious tombs is the mass burials they contain: one held 55 mummy bundles with dead of different ages and sexes (*Fig. 30*). The skulls of several adults showed openings which had partially healed during their lifetime. So far it has not been explained whether these trepannings, which are extremely common on Paracas and Nazca skeletons, were due to war wounds, religious rituals or, as many speculate, to the astonishing skill of the Indian surgeons operating to cure brain disorders.

Only a few hundred yards from these *cavernas* Tello came upon a different type of burial. The graves in what he called the 'Necropolis' consisted of rectangular pits of varying sizes. It has been conjectured that these were the ruins of rooms of much earlier buildings. In these dwellings of the dead lay more than 400 mummy bundles, some of which were about 1.2 m. high and about 1.7 m. in diameter. The majority were somewhat smaller. Many of the 'parcelled' dead sat in baskets, their bodies flexed so as to take up the least possible space, and enveloped in several layers of wrapping (*Fig. 31*). Unlike the *cavernas* corpses, these skulls were artificially elongated and few showed signs of trepanning.

On the basis of the different burial types and grave goods Tello divided the culture into two phases: 'Cavernas', which he took to be earlier, and 'Necropolis', which he believed to be later. Whereas the Cavernas graves were distinguished by splendid ceramic grave goods and the dead were wrapped only in simple gauze-like fabrics, which were rarely decorated with more than two-coloured stripes, the Necropolis corpses displayed dazzling burial cloths or *mantas* (Spanish for a shawl or a royal mantle) and many other splendid fabrics in the numerous layers of the mummy bundles. Rebeca Carrión Cachot examined one of these burial cloths, which are usually about 1 m. wide and 2 m. long, and calculated that it must have taken two years to make.

The dead in these bundles are buried naked in a flexed position. Many wear a few ornaments such as necklaces of shell beads, their body orifices are often covered with

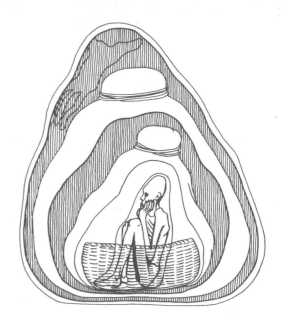

small gold plates, and their heads daubed with red. The method of mummification has not yet been explained. The outer wrapping of the mummy consisted of a simple cotton cloth about 4 m. wide and often as much as 20 m. long. Thanks to these voluminous protective coverings, in conjunction with the saltpetre-rich sand in a desert region, the fantastic motifs and glowing colours of the decorated fabrics have survived in good condition down to the present day.

The cult of the dead was practised to an exceptional degree during this period and in this region. Fabrics of all kinds played a prominent part. They were the medium which helped the living to enter into communication with the powers of the other world and beseech their favour. Between the separate layers of mummy wrappings, at about chest height, lay, carefully folded, several richly ornamented cloths and sumptuous items of clothing – all without the least signs of wear. The 'dowry' of the dead was varied, but extraordinarily rich in comparison with other periods. In some mummy bundles from the Necropolis site there were as many as 150 grave goods made of textiles: tunics, scarves or 'hairnets', headbands, slings, breech clouts, bags, fans and headdresses of every conceivable kind. In addition to cotton, llama and alpaca wool were used, and often agave fibre, while human hair was sometimes spun into the yarn and woven in.

Such are the quality and quantity of textiles of the Necropolis type, i.e. from the Late Paracas and Proto-Nazca phases, that it seems as if the living had devoted themselves solely to spinning and weaving garments for the dead. In the world of the dead nearly every type of weaving known to us is present, in a broad spectrum of some 190 colours and shades of colour. Among the many innovations of spinning, weaving and dyeing techniques made in the Middle and Late phases of the Paracas culture, the cross-knit loop stitch process was particularly important (*Pls. 31, 38, 56, 57*). With this technique, found only in Peru, the weavers gave their textiles a third dimension. The figures in the round of men, birds and fish demons, which look as if they were crocheted, are made of a loop stitch network which lies like a tube around a preformed raw cotton base or thick

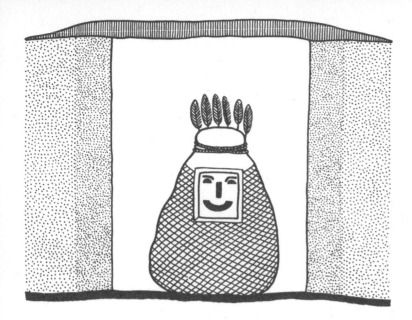

Fig. 32　A mummy bundle in a pit grave displaying a cloth sewn on to serve as a 'protective spirit', and known as a mummy mask (cf. Pls. 11, 40–42). Late Ocucaje phase of the Paracas culture.

Fig. 33　Embroidered border with stylized owl-like birds, Middle or Late Paracas (see Pl. 67).

threads and is sewn onto the base with a few stitches (*Fig. p. 230 (1)*).

The increasingly lavish cult of the dead called on the weavers' greatest talents and took the art of textiles to a peak of creative achievement. As early as the Middle Paracas period, revolutionary technical developments had taken place. The new technique of covering stem stitch embroidery (*Fig. p. 230 (4)*) enabled the weavers to exploit the full possibilities of the dyed wool of alpaca or llama. The first experiments were made in the field of tapestry (weaving with discontinuous weft). Only one Paracas style fabric in tapestry is known (*Pl. 51*): cotton was used for the warp and alpaca for the weft. As the weft need run only over the coloured parts and not over the whole width of the fabric, new wefts for each pattern and colour could be introduced at will; and by alternate looping of the weft threads around a common warp, slits – the natural result of using a discontinuous weft – could be avoided (*Fig. p. 230 (2)*). Fertile imagination in the details now produced a great variety of patterns. The lavishness of 'Paracas-Necropolis' art is found only rarely in later periods.

Tello's typology of 'Paracas-Cavernas' and 'Paracas-Necropolis' was accepted for decades, but recent excavations and a growing body of material sold by *huaqueros* to private collectors has led to a reassessment of Paracas culture, and to a more detailed stylistic and chronological subdivision. The main sites yielding Paracas material range from the Ica valley in the north to the river system of the Rio Grande de Nazca in the south with Cahuachi as its centre. It is now unanimously accepted that the Paracas culture combined two different traditions which overlapped in time. One, with typical Chavín elements, was largely formed by outside influences (hence the term 'Chavinoid Paracas'), while the other appears to be a mainly localized indigenous development. The Nazca culture grew out of this indigenous tradition.

The chief method of establishing the chronology of successive cultures is the stylistic analysis of ceramics. Fired clay was the material most experimented with in ancient Peru and therefore most responsive to cultural change. The weaver's art was more

conservative, and it is often difficult to classify textiles chronologically, or even stylistically, without recourse to pottery. The Paracas culture, which inaugurated a new era in textile production with an amazing display of colours, is an exception. New religious ideas are expressed by brilliantly coloured mythical beings which animate the surface of the fabrics as if they were floating in the air. In textiles the differences between the two cultural traditions are clearly visible. The people of Chavín found new forms for their gods by fusing animal and human elements, thus taking the figures out of the realm of reality and creating an unbridgeable distance between god and man. The eyes, which create the contact between divine image and beholder, are animal eyes, searching, uncanny, frightening. The Paracas artists depict felines in profile, only the head being shown frontally. This gives the impression that the animal had just spotted the beholder and frozen momentarily, fixing him with a penetrating stare (*Fig. 35*).

The Oculate Being, its smiling fangless face no longer reminiscent of the Chavín feline, now becomes the centre of more complicated representations. The textile pattern in *Figure 37* shows this figure, with snakes emerging from its head, depicted in a peculiar frontal view; the body, presented in profile, encloses another creature, and all the interstices are filled with miniature cats, just as in the period of the 'little kingdoms', and indeed down to the time of the Incas.

The Paracas artists clothed their gods in magnificent costumes and conceived fantastic masks for their heads. Yet the relaxed, floating quality which Paracas figures seem to radiate is deceptive: their clothing and their dance-like postures distract attention from the central theme of these representations, which is the severed head of an enemy. Generally the figures hold a trophy head in one hand and weapons in the other (*Pl. 63*) – the *tumi* or crescent-shaped ceremonial knife, arrows and throwing sticks, spears and *bolas* (a throwing weapon made of rope attached to stones). The accompanying ornament and the many images and symbols of growing plants and fruit in combination with trophy heads leave no doubt that the people of that culture saw in the severed head of

an enemy the magic power required to appease and nourish the vegetation gods who demanded human sacrifice.

On a woollen fabric border a vegetation god with skull-like head and ape-like limbs holding a trophy head is depicted in covering stem stitch embroidery (*Pl. 68*). From the blood flowing from this freshly severed head sprout the stems of fruit-bearing plants (beans and chili peppers, both basic foods of the ancient Peruvians). At the same time, this embroidery expresses the old Indian concept that man is the 'nourisher and preserver' of the gods, that he must give them strength, even by spilling human blood, in order to maintain the cosmic order. These gods, the embodiment of natural forces, were looked on as omnipotent, demonic and unpredictable. Convincing evidence of how closely the ancient Peruvians associated their desire for the fields to be fertile with the appeasement of the gods by human sacrifice through the trophy head cult is also found in Nazca art. Thousands of years after their disappearance, the people of that ancient tradition and their world of ideas come alive for us through their textiles.

It is only recently that the fabrics found in graves have been thought worth preserving. In the case of early finds, mostly from grave robberies, gold and silver were the main objectives: until the mid-twentieth century, fabrics were thrown away as unmarketable. Today, however, textiles have taken their place alongside other material as valuable clues to the understanding of ancient Peruvian life and religion. Even so, little notice has so far been taken of their value in understanding the different social and political structures of the great Central Andean cultures.

There seems to have been no clear-cut social division by classes in the Chavinoid Paracas and Early Paracas phases. One obvious indication of important changes in the economic sphere is the large number of sites with Middle and Late Paracas material which lie not near the coast but in river valleys further inland: clearly the sea was no longer the main source of food. Nearly all the agricultural products that were to be important later as well – chiefly maize – seem to have been first established on the coast.

Fig. 36 An anthropomorphic cat whose tail turns into a jagged snake with a trophy head, from a Paracas embroidery.

The farmers in the river valleys probably increased the productivity of their fields by artificial irrigation. Clear traces of an irrigation system have been found at Chavín de Huántar, and similar installations are known at several south coast sites. The long periods over which they were used – some are still in use today – as well as frequent improvements and changes make their archaeological classification extremely difficult. The development of an irrigation system, the establishment of a strong political leadership, and the emergence of centralized organization are to some degree connected. Improved agriculture led to a marked population increase, concentrated in the fertile zones along the rivers in the interior. As there is virtually no rainfall in this region and the rivers descending from the mountains are the sole source of water, the people had to divert the river into canals and lead it to their fields, and that was only possible by well-organized communal work under strong leadership.

How did questions of productivity, specialization of craft work and social stratification affect textiles? A weaver needed 85 m. of yarn for one of the simple cotton strips, usually 50×15 cm., of the kind produced even before the Early Horizon. A normal shirt 1 m. long and 45 cm. wide consisted of 6 such strips, i.e. 510 m. of yarn. If we allot a man of the Preceramic Period three such simple items of clothing, a burial shirt and two shirts for everyday wear, he needed at least 1,530 m. of cotton yarn. If we take the lower estimate of the population of Huaca Prieta (200–400), 200 people needed at least 306 km. of yarn for clothing and about 150 km. for fishing nets, ropes and other items of everyday use. If we take a big leap through space and time from the little fishing settlement of the Preceramic Period in the North to the Paracas Necropolis, the 'city of the dead' at the beginning of the Early Intermediate period, we find that even the simplest cotton cloths are much better and more tightly woven. We can assume an average of 8 warp threads and 8 weft threads per square centimetre of plain weave fabric. That means one square metre would contain 800 m. of warp and weft threads. For the production of a normal cloth of 20×4 m., of the kind used for the outer

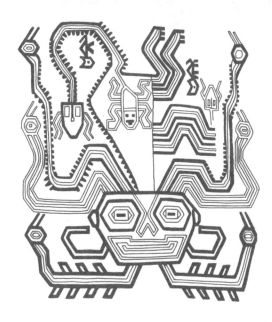

Fig. 37   A cat, transformed into the Oculate Being by its enormous eyes, joined with snakes to form a composite creature. From a Paracas embroidered border. (Textile Museum, Washington, D.C.)

wrapping of a mummy bundle, the weavers needed 156.8 km. of cotton yarn, i.e. more than half the population of Huaca Prieta needed for all their clothing, including 'the last shirt'. If we then take into account the other cloths in the bundle, we have to conclude that more yarn was needed for a single burial than for several hundred living persons of earlier generations. If we carry these calculations further and remember that Tello found 55 mummy bundles in one Cavernas grave and a tomb with as many as 429 on the Necropolis site, we arrive at a length of yarn that would go several times round the Equator. Such a consumption could only be guaranteed by extensive high-yielding cotton fields, and they in turn required efficient irrigation systems.

Variations in the ways the dead were treated indicate the power of individuals and their prestige in the community, status and position being directly related to possessions and the quality and quantity of textile grave goods. It is now clear that there was an élite at the head of society which exercised religious and political power. What is striking is not only the increasing importance of the cult of the dead, but also its association with the trophy head cult. The type of religious cult practised on the South Coast, especially the great ceremonial importance of human trophy heads for agricultural rites, clearly shows that the power and claim to power of the priests and the chieftains were based largely on secular and military considerations. Similar symptoms are recognizable after the collapse of the Chavín culture on the Central and South Coast – the formation of secularly oriented societies under the leadership of chieftains with limited localized territorial claims mostly connected with the struggle for water.

For a long time the archaeological picture of the Paracas culture contained no clues to its religious, political or economic centres. Until the mid-1950s what was known of Nazca architecture was not comparable to the large structures from the same period in the North of Peru. The extensive burial sites in the deserts along the Rio Grande de Nazca and the other river valleys of the South Coast bear witness to a comparatively large population, and the old view that no villages or settlements existed on Paracas-Nazca

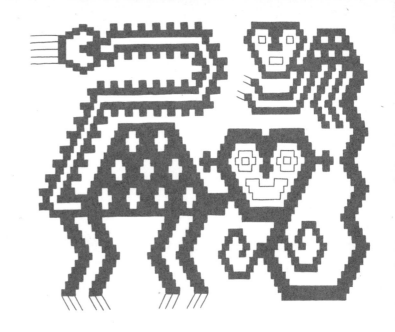

Fig. 38 Embroidery pattern on an unfinished Paracas burial cloth. The main figure may be seen to represent a priest, with 'mouth mask' (cp. Pl. 73) and headdress. A snake's body ending in a cat's head flows upward from his mouth like a speech scroll. (After a drawing by Junius B. Bird of a cloth in the Textile Museum, Washington, D. C.)

Fig. 39 A monkey-like creature and its young, combined into a single pattern on a Paracas embroidered border. The tail represents a jagged snake.

territory has now been definitely abandoned. W. Duncan Strong even went so far as to claim that the remains of masonry of sun-dried conical mud bricks (*adobes*) and traces of streets which he and other scholars excavated on the terrain of the Hacienda Cahuachi were the remains of a city.

Evidence of urban and ceremonial architecture has also been discovered in other valleys, yet Cahuachi is still unique: no other site has been so thoroughly studied by experts. According to existing evidence it was inhabited from the Early Horizon (Middle Paracas) down to the Early Intermediate Period (Early Nazca). The precise extent of Cahuachi is very hard to determine, because the houses, as was usual in this arid zone, were built of wattle and reed, so that virtually nothing has survived above ground level. Strong found both Cavernas and Necropolis type ceramics at Cahuachi. Both often coexist in the same level, and within one burial ground. This goes against Tello's theory that Cavernas was early and Necropolis later. Beneath the great temple of Cahuachi, on its western side, Strong came across a virtual warehouse of cotton cloth of the kind used for the mummy bundles on the Necropolis site. A cloth that was 7 m. wide and had the astonishing length of more than 50 m. lay in a tomb 18 m. long by 1.7 m. wide. It was in a single piece and not rolled but carefully folded concertina fashion. No large burial chambers or pit graves were found, and only a few skulls with deformation similar to those of the Cavernas graves came to light.

But even if there is no significant chronological gap between these (in Tello's view) quite dissimilar cultures, is there perhaps a social gap? Were the precious cloths reserved exclusively for members of an upper class? We do not know. Chronologically speaking, the new finds have shown Tello's Paracas-Cavernas phase to be a regional stylistic variation of Middle Paracas in which the indigenous tradition that introduced the trophy head cult was given expression. Paracas-Necropolis corresponds to Late Paracas and Proto-Nazca in the chronological table.[12] Yet the transition in arts and crafts from Middle Paracas to Proto-Nazca, a period of nearly five hundred years, is

fluid. After the fading of Chavín characteristics a major break is no longer perceptible. One style intermingles with the other in the search for new means of expression. The material for this experimental stage on sites known to us is so varied that even the normally informative ceramics do not tell a consistent story. When it comes to textiles, which have mostly reached us as fragments and without an archaeological context, attribution to a precise stylistic phase (Middle Paracas, Late Paracas or Proto-Nazca) is even more difficult. The chemist Salzmann found the only reliable clue in the red dye used at the time. According to him, the artists of the Paracas culture made their red from the shell of a bivalve, *Choncholopa*, whereas the dye for Nazca fabrics was obtained from the cochineal beetle.

The Nazca culture takes its name from the provincial capital of the Ica Department. Its sphere of influence corresponds roughly to that of the Paracas culture, with the exception of the South, where its influence extended into the valley of the Acari river. We have no idea what language was spoken in either the Nazca or the Paracas culture, but it was probably the same, because there is no indication of an ethnic change or a mass migration. An alien people would scarcely have been able to accept the religious ideas so completely or follow them up so logically as the Nazca did. But unlike Paracas, the main medium of the Nazca culture was not textiles but painted pottery.

The struggle for liberation from the Chavín gods led to numerous creative experiments in Paracas, many of them lacking a transcendental or numinous dimension and being if anything all too human. In the Early Nazca phase, painted pottery chiefly shows motifs with figures belonging to the agrarian religion as depicted on Paracas fabrics (*Figs. 40, 41*). But the most striking feature is the trophy head: the severed head of an enemy in the hands of priests and warriors, a central theme on Paracas fabrics, becomes even more emphatically the main motif of Nazca mythology, whether on clay vessels (*Figs. 42, 43*) or on surviving textiles (*Pls. 60, 68, 69*).

Looking at these images, we cannot help asking where all the severed heads came

Figs. 40, 41   The cat as 'bringer of food', on a Paracas painted cloth (right) and a Nazca vase painting (left).

from that were considered so indispensable to make the crops thrive and propitiate the gods. This brings us back to the fact that we are dealing with people for whom the struggle for water was basic. When large families and especially tribal groups led by chieftains fought each other for the precious liquid no quarter was given or expected. The victors gained both water for their fields and severed heads to ensure the favour of the gods (*Pl. 62*).

The numerous finds of carefully prepared and elaborately decorated trophy heads recovered from Late Paracas and Nazca graves confirm that they were believed to confer supernatural powers. In many heads still preserved in good condition today, the eyes are covered with pieces of silver or shells, a strip of sheet gold protects the nose, and a *bolas* is wrapped round as a headdress. Other heads were specially dressed for burial: the face, for instance, might be covered with an extremely fine fabric on which feathers from tropical birds are sewn (*Pl. 74*).

A feature already noted in Paracas motifs is also applicable to Nazca designs. There is always a naturalistic element inherent in the gods and demons, no matter how abstract they may be, and the artists in whose imagination these creatures originated can never quite conceal this human aspect. But in the Nazca phase, the iconography of the world of gods and demons is more mature. Amid all the baroque wealth of detail, one finds a very subtle manner of representation. The specific attributes of the mythical beings are a kind of explanatory key to the sense and meaning of what is represented. To some extent Early Nazca art harks back to the old religious concepts of Chavín, but the manifold world of gods and demons is reduced to a single figure, the 'Cat Demon', a mythical creature combining human and animal features and equipped, in highly symbolic imagery, with the most important attributes of the fertility cult. Eduard Seler called this hybrid 'the bringer of food'. As the 'god with the mouth mask' we also encounter it in many representations where it is characterized by a nose ornament which imitates a cat's whiskers.

Figs. 42, 43   The 'bringer of food', depicted on Nazca ceramics. The trophy heads in its claws and decorating its robes indicate the sacrifice the god demands from man. (After Alan R. Sawyer)

This 'mouth mask' appears on Paracas fabrics (*Fig. 38*) more frequently than in Nazca art (*Figs. 42, 43*). A beaten gold nose ornament in the form of the 'feline mouth mask' (*Pl. 73*), found in a grave, must originally have belonged to a Nazca priest who would have worn it in his lifetime during religious ceremonies. Similar artefacts made of other materials help us to interpret the images and symbols which we find on textiles such as a Proto-Nazca embroidery (*Pl. 44*). An interesting thing about the nose ornament is that the whiskers end in snake heads. In other words, the snake retains the character as a fertility symbol that it had in the Chavín culture. A similar combination of snake and feline is seen in the Proto-Nazca embroidery. Here a dignitary appears dressed as a fertility demon in a ceremonial mask with snakes; his hair takes the form of long snakes hanging down to the ground, with stylized sprouting fruits issuing from their mouths, and the ceremonial staff has the form of a double-headed snake. The connection with the old fertility cult represented by the snake is unmistakable. Finally, basic features of the Chavín gods are also perpetuated in the 'Cat Demon', which appears in various disguises, mostly birds' plumage (*Figs. 42, 43*), as ruler of the winds and simultaneously as bringer of fertility.

We sometimes find other highly stylized gods and animals in the coastal region. Puma and jaguar are replaced by otters and small felines, for example, and the eagle and condor of the highlands by the falcon. This is obviously a local development, a transformation of the terrifying Chavín ideology to suit the local and more provincial conditions on the South Coast. The people of the Nazca culture also worshipped an imaginary creature with the face of a beast of prey, framed by jagged staffs which must also be snake attributes – the 'jagged staff demon' (*Figs. 13, 14*). The jagged snake already appeared on embroidered Paracas borders (*Figs. 36, 37, 39*).

Even though the patterns of the Nazca period exhibit an independent style in many ways, it is interesting that here too we find fabric patterns which, like the representations of the Chavín culture, are intended to be looked at from different angles. The fabric

Fig. 44 Tapestry pattern in Nazca-Huari style. The double-headed puma, the highland god, is combined with toads or tadpoles, representing water – a mixture that indicates the increasing influence of Highland culture on the South Coast.

44 A dignitary in cult costume, perhaps a priest, wearing the 'feline mouth mask' – part of a border embroidered in covering stem stitch. Late Paracas/ Proto-Nazca, c. 300–100 BC.

in *Plate 71*, for example, shows the head of a mythical creature with a headdress which, turned upside down, is repeated, not with a deliberately different facial expression, but simply in another colour. We find really bizarre creatures on fabrics with the 'diver' motif (*Pl. 58*). An exceptional phenomenon in the final Nazca phase is patchwork (*Pl. 78*), made by sewing together many brightly coloured patches with geometric patterns produced by a relatively sophisticated dyeing technique – *plangi*, or tie-dyeing – rare in ancient Peru. In the textile motifs of the Highland culture of the Middle Horizon – the Huari culture which spread throughout Peru in the second half of the first millennium and even influenced the indigenous Nazca style (*Fig. 44*) – every detail is once again subordinated to a rigorous creative principle.

45

46

45 *A fragment of a border embroidered with demonic masks in covering stem stitch. Middle Paracas, c. 500–300 BC.*

46 *Characteristic feline motifs in covering stem stitch embroidery on a burial cloth. Middle–Late Paracas, c. 500–200 BC.*

47

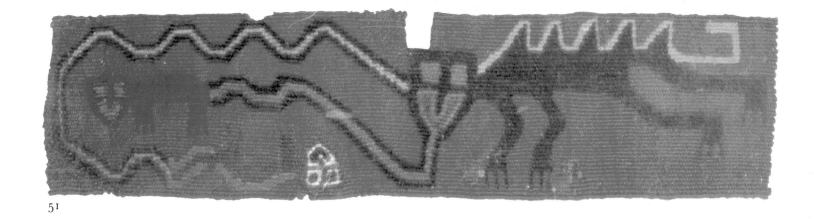

51

48, 49 *Five borders from robes or burial mantles, embroidered in covering stem stitch. Late Paracas/Proto-Nazca, c.300–100 BC.*

50 *Part of a border in covering stem stitch showing two inter- twined snakes with lizards and mice. Late Paracas, c.300–200 BC.*

51 *Probably the earliest sur- viving example of tapestry weaving – a fragment on which different figures are connected to form a single mythical being. Late Paracas/Proto-Nazca, c.300–100 BC.*

52, 53 *Three borders embroi- dered in covering stem stitch with birds and fish. Late Paracas, c.500–200 BC.*

52   53

54

54 The 'grinning monkey demon' surrounded by jagged
snakes and flanked by 'atten-
dant spirits', embroidered in
stem stitch. Middle–Late
Paracas, c. 500–200 BC.

55 Cotton fabric with designs
painted in dark brown. Late
Paracas/Proto-Nazca,
c. 300–100 BC.

56 Two faces from an ornamental border, embroidered in
cross-knit loop stitch. Late
Paracas/Proto-Nazca,
c. 300–100 BC.

55

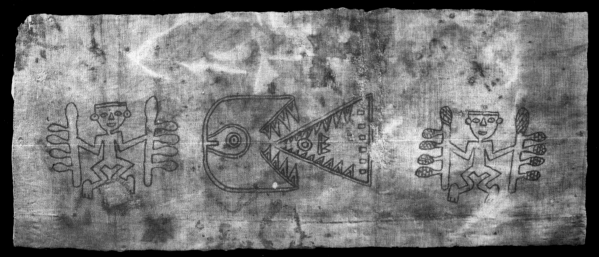

56

57 *Part of the decorative trim-ming used to edge a burial cloth. The cross-knit loop stitch em-broidery includes dancing figures. Proto-Nazca–Early Nazca, c. 200 BC–AD 200.*

57

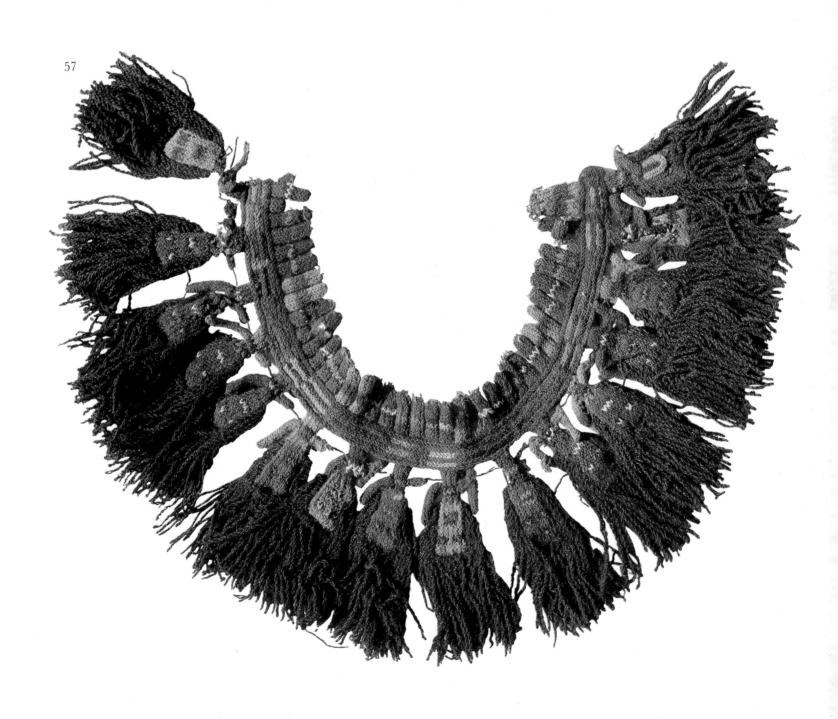

58

59

59

58, 59 *Similar motifs, from borders embroidered in covering stem stitch. The upper 'diver' or 'falling figure' may, with its exposed ribs, represent a sacrificial victim. The lower one has been seen as a 'dancing' warrior or warlike deity, holding a throwing stick and* tumi. *Late Paracas/Proto-Nazca, c. 300–100 BC.*

60 *A border design of similar technique and date showing a deity clutching a trophy head and avid for sacrificial victims.*

60

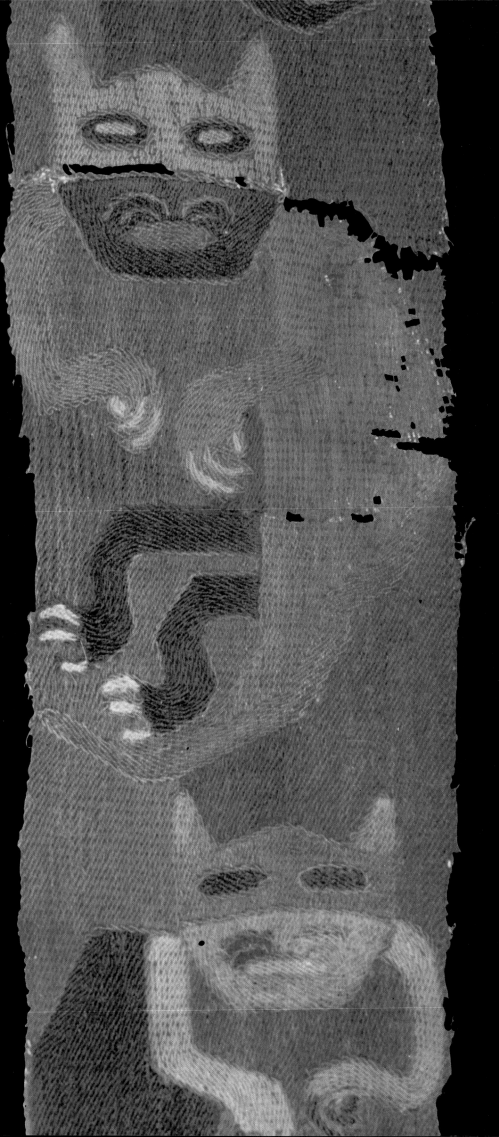

61 *Fabulous feline creatures on a border embroidered in covering stem stitch. Late Paracas/ Proto-Nazca, c. 300–100 BC.*

62 *Two warriors holding weapons and trophy heads, from an embroidered fabric. Late Paracas/Proto-Nazca, c. 300–100 BC.*

Overleaf:

63 *Covering stem stitch embroidery depicting a vegetation god with human features and the limbs of a monkey. A snake's body flows from its mouth like a speech scroll. Late Paracas/ Proto-Nazca, c. 300–100 BC.*

62

64 *A priest or warrior in the ceremonial costume of a 'bird man', from an embroidered border. Late Paracas/Proto-Nazca, c. 300–100 BC.*

65 *A dancing warrior, shown in the imposing stance of a 'man of action' – a subject characteristic of a late Necropolis variation within Paracas textiles. From a Late Paracas/Proto-Nazca border embroidered in covering stem stitch, c. 300–100 BC.*

66 *Embroidered pattern band; several of the motifs – animals and hybrid creatures – are unfinished. Late Paracas/Proto-Nazca, c. 300–100 BC.*

67 *A bird, perhaps an owl demon, from a border embroidered in covering stem stitch. Middle–Late Paracas, c. 500–200 BC.*

68 *A vegetation god with skull-like head and simian limbs, wearing a wing-like cloak consisting of two snakes' bodies. His garments are decorated with heads, and he holds a severed head from which blood streams out and turns into plants. From a border embroidered in stem stitch. Late Paracas/Proto-Nazca, c. 300–100 BC.*

67

69 *Part of a burial cloth, embroidered with anthropomorphic winged demons, who have feline features and hold trophy heads. Late Paracas/Proto-Nazca, c. 300–100 BC.*

70, 71 *Two slit tapestries depicting a Nazca deity. The lower image in the shape of a head is repeated, upside down, in different colours. Nazca, c. AD 100–600.*

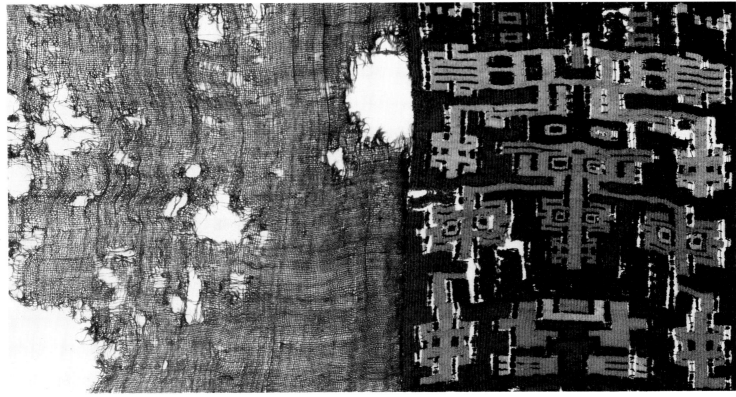

70

71

72 *Double spout vessel with polychrome painting of a feline deity shown with the 'feline mouth mask'. Nazca, c. AD 100–600.*

73 *A nose ornament of sheet gold, contemporary with the vessel in Pl. 72, representing the 'feline mouth mask' and probably worn by a dignitary during religious ceremonies.*

74 *Two actual trophy heads, covered with featherwork on which facial features and ornaments of gold and silver sheet are sewn. Nazca-Huari, c. 600–700.*

72

73

75, 77 *A cloth, probably originally part of a wall-hanging. Cross-shaped patterns enclosing mythical birds and stylized trophy heads are woven in tapestry on a plain weave ground of alpaca wool almost as fine as gauze. Nazca-Huari, c.600–700.*

76 *Fragment of an* unku *in tapestry technique, with realistic lobsters in a geometrical framework. Late Nazca, Huari influence, c.600–700.*

76

75

77

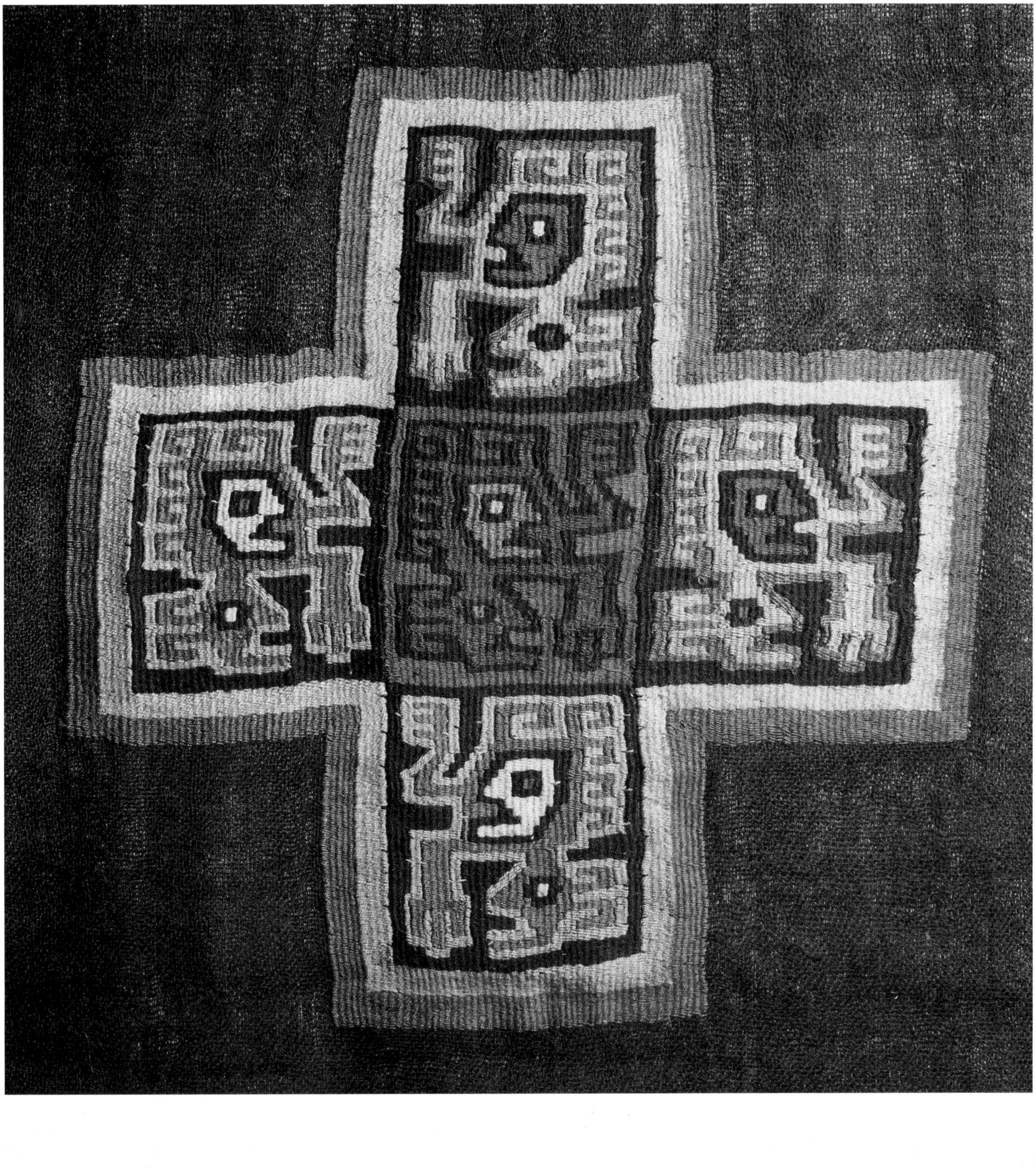

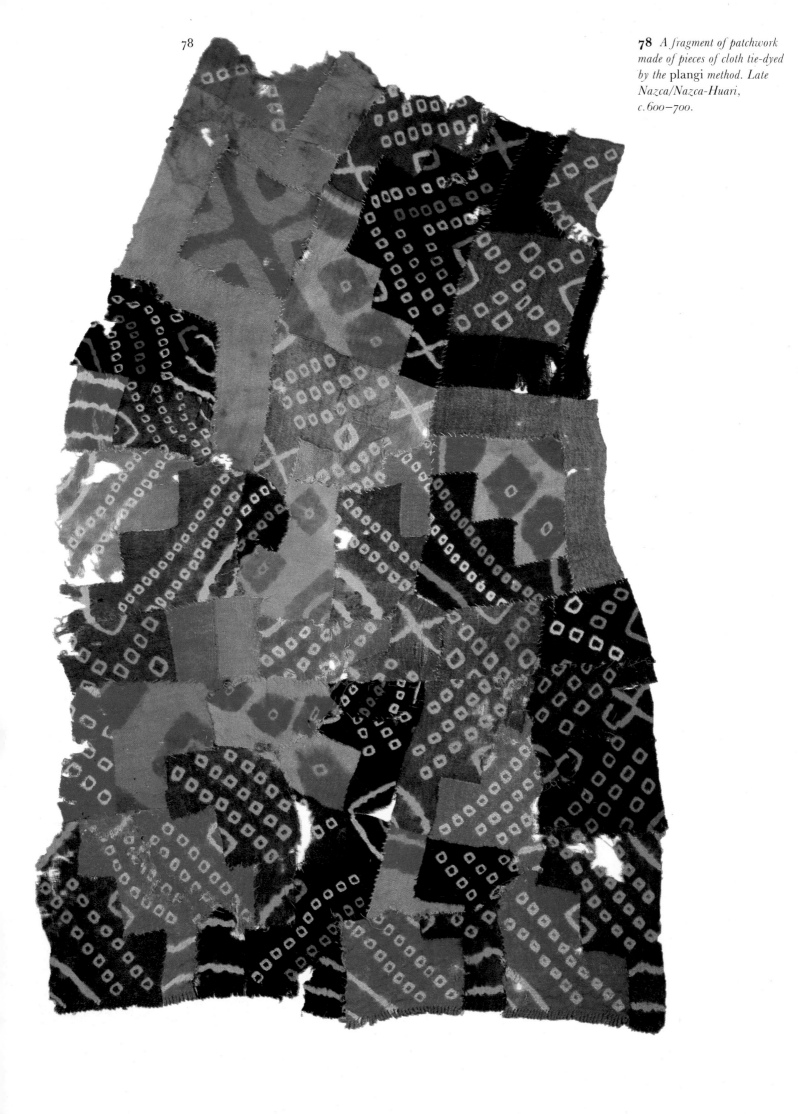

From Naturalism to Abstraction

4

The tightest hand-woven textiles ever made, surpassing even eighteenth-century Brussels tapestries, come from the Middle Horizon. Some of them, through the beauty of their colour composition and the boldness of their design, belong among the great masterpieces of world art. The perfection with which the weavers transferred the religious motifs found on stone reliefs to textiles indicates a Highland origin, as does the clothing type – a wide poncho-like mantle, ideal for the harsh climate, reaching from the shoulders to the knees and made from one piece of cloth sewn together on both sides leaving slits for the arms. The basic pattern of the tapestry fabrics usually consists of a highly abstract figure composed of many individual elements broken up into cube-like forms, which seems at first sight purely ornamental. To grasp the significance of the iconography of this specific pattern, we must call on a stone relief to provide the key – the 'Gateway of the Sun' at Tiahuanaco (*Pl. 80; Fig. 46*).

The Tiahuanaco culture, from which the style known by many Americanists today as 'Middle Horizon' is ultimately derived, began in the Southern Highlands, on the vast *altiplano* 4,000 m. above sea level. Faced with the endless bleak expanse of these rocky highlands and fascinated by the powerful forces of nature, the indigenous Indians developed their own world-picture, from which the striking features and great expressive power of their art derive. The mentality of the highland Indian thus differed from that of the coastal population. The harsh mountain climate, with icy winds from dusk to dawn, and a burning treacherous sun at midday, produced a withdrawn, introspective type of people, fanatical and stubborn. In spite of this, the Peruvian-Bolivian *altiplano* is still one of the most densely populated areas in both countries. Two Indian languages, Aymara, and the old imperial tongue of the Incas, Quechua, which every year advances further into Aymara-speaking territory, predominate here.[13]

The region around Lake Titicaca, with an area of some 8,200 square kilometres, in the incomparable setting of its permanently snow-clad mountains, some as high as 6,000 m., is considered to be one of the most beautiful places in the world. But at the

Figs. 45, 46 A schematic drawing of the central figure on the Gateway of the Sun at Tiahuanaco (Pl. 80) shows that while its costume and attributes (condor – redrawn, left – and feline, snakes, etc.) are similar to those of the Chavín Staff God (Fig. 21), it is much more recognizably a human figure.

same time it is a district which makes heavy demands on its inhabitants. Today, as in the remote past, the Aymara farmers cultivate their fields, sowing and harvesting the same crops – many species of potatoes and a few other plants such as *oca* and *quinoa* that still thrive at this altitude. Indeed, in some places protected from the wind, they have even managed to adapt a special type of maize to the harsh climate. Fish from the small streams and big lakes supplement their diet.

Apart from the Quechua-speakers, the Aymara were the only Indian pastoral people in the pre-Spanish period. Their ancestors bred alpacas and llamas even in ancient times, and it was mainly the wool of these two animals that supported their intensive trade with the inhabitants of the coast. From about the middle of the first millennium AD, these commercial relations also helped the religious and artistic ideas of the highlanders to penetrate into the coastal region. In addition to ceramics, the forceful multi-coloured textile patterns expressing religious ideas were instrumental in spreading the Tiahuanaco ideology over large areas of ancient Peru. The final phase of the Middle Horizon is characterized by a more or less successful fusion of the old motifs, by now unintelligible, with local stylistic variations better suited to the more flexible mentality of the coast dwellers.

During the first centuries AD, certain religious ideas and stylistic peculiarities crystallized near the small village of Tiahuanaco in present-day Bolivia on the south shore of Lake Titicaca. The Tiahuanaco culture was given a more secular expression at Huari, further to the north but still in the Southern Highlands, near the city of Ayacucho in Peru. Between the sixth and seventh centuries, stylistic changes begin with the spread of this Huari culture (probably the result in most cases of a politico-military expansion by the Aymara) in the Central Highlands and on the coast. But the stylistic elements which originated in Tiahuanaco and Huari continued to nourish the art of the central Andes region, with the exception of Ecuador, for centuries.

Parallel with these gradual stylistic changes in art came new social and political

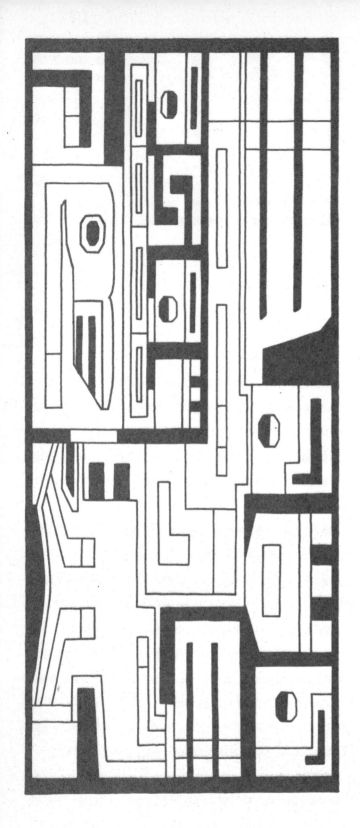

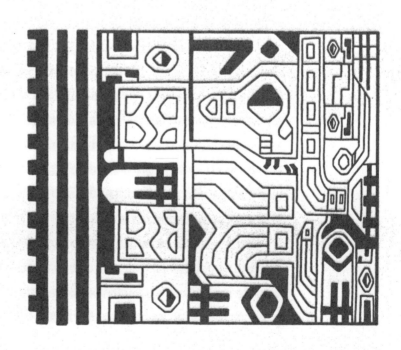

Figs. 50–52 Stylized versions of the condor-headed staff-bearer on the Gateway of the Sun at Tiahuanaco (Fig. 53), from ornamental bands on garments in Tiahuanaco-Huari style preserved in graves on the South Coast. (Fig. 50 after Alan R. Sawyer)

Fig. 53 Staff-bearer with a condor head, on the frieze of the Gateway of the Sun at Tiahuanaco.

have upturned birds' heads (*Fig. 53*), while in the upper and lower rows they have human heads with remarkably sharp noses (*Fig. 57*). Even in the most extreme abstraction on fabrics with the diagonal double motif this pointed nose still appears as a distinctive ingredient (*Fig. 65*). Common to both groups of staff-bearers is a garment with wings whose individual feathers, like the ceremonial staffs, end sometimes in birds' and sometimes in fishes' heads.

Without having the model of these clearly represented figures on the frieze of the Gateway of the Sun, in which everything is subject to strict stylistic and formal laws and every detail is relevant and symbolically important, it would be virtually impossible to recognize the symbolism of the figures in Tiahuanaco-Huari style fabrics, let alone to interpret them. It is as if the message of the reliefs had been translated into a secret code in the fabrics. Much still remains uncertain. The pattern of the tapestry in *Plate 105*, for example, which consists of several semi-human, semi-feline heads, has led to speculation that it might be a system of writing or calendar signs, because of the arrangement in fields, the varied geometric headdresses and facial painting, and the complicated colour scheme. But so far no proof of this has been forthcoming.

A great number of Middle Horizon textiles have been found, almost all in burials (as with other ancient Peruvian textiles). They have been called 'tapestries', because of a resemblance to the finest European tapestries, but strictly speaking the technique involved is plain weave rep with concealed warp, that is, the warp is completely covered by the weft; where different colours meet, the wefts, or supplementary yarns, are interlaced or looped alternately around a common warp to avoid slits (*Fig. p. 230 (4)*). Occasionally the wefts are not interlocked, resulting in slit tapestries.

The works recovered from graves not only show that there were outstanding weavers among the people: they also enable us to recognize differences of rank more clearly than in other cultures. For unlike the *mantas*, the precious grave cloths of the Paracas and Nazca cultures, many of the Tiahuanaco-Huari items of clothing show signs of wear.

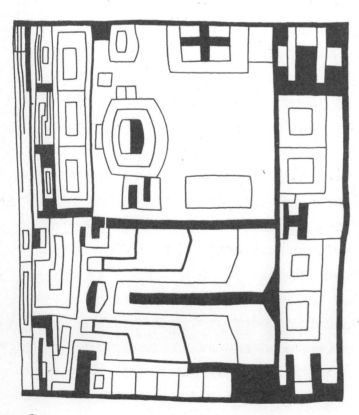

Fig.54   *Staff-bearer with feline head and markings, from a vase painting.*

Figs.55, 56   *The same motif, broken down into angular forms, from fabrics in Tiahuanaco-Huari style.*

Fig.57   *Staff-bearer with a human head on the Gateway of the Sun at Tiahuanaco.*

Evidently they only became burial shirts or mummy wrappings after they had already been worn by the living. The technical quality and careful composition of colours and motifs on many ponchos suggest an 'official' garment for higher dignitaries.

Something of a return to the old Chavín concept is also demonstrable in the Middle Horizon. The feline, the bird of prey, the fish and the snake still retain divine status. It is only the actual artistic style that differs. The limited iconography of the fabrics characteristic of the Middle Horizon centres around the elements that we know from the frieze on the Gateway of the Sun, whose anthropomorphic figures arouse distant memories of the Raimondi Stele from the Chavín period (*Fig. 21*), a resemblance reinforced by the fact that the superior beings of the Chavín period also hold a ceremonial staff in their hands. Yet unlike the Chavín style, with its elegant volute-like lines, the severe Tiahuanaco style prefers a strict rectangularity. In its classic expression, even curving natural forms are compressed into geometric shapes. The ceramic art of the period also obeys this canon. If the outline of a vessel makes it impossible for artists to avoid curves and bulges, they try to counteract these by severity of line and rigid geometric forms (*Pls. 81–85*). The technique of weaving, especially slit tapestry, was far more suited to this austere kind of design. And yet the abstraction that is so striking in the Tiahuanaco-Huari style is not really governed by the requirements of the weaving process: it is a consciously introduced stylistic device. In the course of the centuries, the basic patterns remained dominant, but with their increasing breakdown into rectilinear forms, they turned into almost pure ornament. The reproduction of natural forms was completely banished from every kind of religious representation.

We can only guess at the reasons for this deliberate transformation of natural models into abstract geometric forms. Perhaps the Indians thought it was wrong to represent divine beings in the guise of earthly creatures. To primitive people natural phenomena are not explicable as they are to us by physical or chemical laws. In the overpowering environment of the Central Andes, the unpredictable variations in the fertility of the

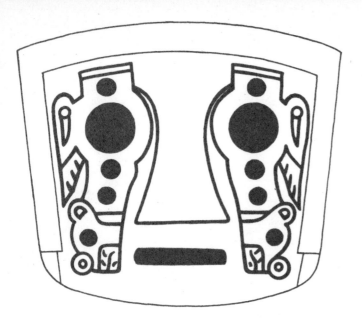

Fig.58 The tearmarks on the face of the central figure on the Gateway of the Sun at Tiahuanaco are an essential difference between it and the Chavín Staff God.

fields, the mysterious movements of the stars and the more violent acts of nature were inexplicable. Everything that happened or did not happen they looked on as the work of their gods alone. The fact that when natural forms were transferred to textile decoration they were literally 'deconstructed' is no doubt due to a deliberate intention to express the incomprehensible by going as far as possible away from reality.

Figures 61, 62 and *65* show a pattern on textiles and on ceramic which can only be interpreted by reference to the symbolic representations on the frieze of the Gateway of the Sun, which are still based on natural models. Here the same motifs are taken to an extreme of abstraction. The human face is reduced to individual signs – the eye with its tearmark is shown frontally, while the pointed nose and horseshoe-shaped mouth are depicted in side view, all transposed to the flat surface in a carefully balanced manner – signs used for centuries to make up decorative patterns which to the Indians of the time were meaningful, expressive and imaginatively stimulating.

Alan Sawyer has divided Tiahuanaco style textiles into three groups according to their motifs and compositional characteristics. The first group is that of the staff-bearers or 'staff-bearing figures', typified by representations of the god and the 'genii' which seem to have been transferred directly from the Gateway of the Sun to textiles, though in abstract form (*Figs.50–52, 55, 56*). The second is that of the diagonal double motif or 'paired elements': two elements are paired within a rectangle divided by a diagonal, and arranged in registers of alternating orientation (*Figs.61, 62, 65*). The third group is that of the composite motif. Here four or eight abstract figural elements are combined in rectangular fields in such a way that they produce a new image. *Figure 63* shows how by the combination of two highly stylized birds' heads in profile arranged horizontally (one light, one dark) a front-view human face is formed, its wide mouth made up of the two birds' beaks meeting at the central axis.

Perhaps the extraordinary evocative power that emanates from Tiahuanaco style textiles is actually due to their magical stylization. Not even the Inca style exercised

Fig. 59 A schematic redrawing of part of a tapestry fragment (Pl. 105), showing six of the many heads. Three of these show the ritual face-painting with tearmarks. The alternate heads have no such marks, and probably represent skulls. A similar distinction may be indicated by the depiction of the 'divided eyes', which are sometimes divided vertically (the living?) and sometimes horizontally (the dead?).

quite such a far-reaching and profound influence as did the Tiahuanaco style in its late Huari phase, when it spread throughout Peru. By the beginning of the eighth century BC Tiahuanaco influence had established itself everywhere. Regional styles were pushed back or assimilated, especially on the South Coast. New stimuli for craft work came mainly from a combination of the declining but still expressive Nazca style – which was to some extent related to the Tiahuanaco-Huari style by its marked abstraction – with Highland elements (*Fig. 44*).

The Tiahuanaco-Huari expansion proved less artistically productive on the North Coast, formerly the home of the Moche culture whose heyday was long since over. Here was the meeting of two obviously incompatible currents, entirely different in style and basic content: the stylizing abstract 'cubist' art of the Tiahuanaco phase and the realistic secular art of the Mochica (*Pls. 7, 8*).

The Moche civilization, which flourished at the same time as the Nazca but several hundred kilometres to the north, has left no significant surviving textiles. (For that reason it was not discussed with contemporary developments in the previous chapter.) Though we know from representations on Mochica pottery that textiles played an important role (*Fig. 5*), it seems they did not achieve the artistic quality and colouring of those woven in the south. From the few wool and cotton fragments that have been salvaged from the damper climate of the north, and from realistic depictions on vessels (*Fig. 67*) and ceramic sculpture (*Pl. 7*), we can build up a fairly accurate picture of Moche costume. Humble farmers and craftsmen, as well as women, wore a shirt reaching almost to the knee, usually decorated with a few geometric patterns. The ruler's shirts were more richly patterned and were made up of different woven cloths stitched together. Often additional ornaments were attached in the form of small copper or gold plaques and fringes. Even the Mochica's headgear is known from ceramic painting and sculpture. The men's consisted of a turban and the women's of a long cloth hanging down their backs. The headdresses of the élite were extremely varied and indicated the

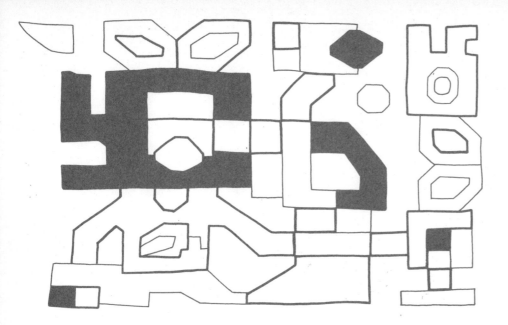

Fig.60 The staff-bearer motif transformed by weavers unfamiliar with the rigid iconography of the classic Tiahuanaco style. This drawing interprets the pattern on a tapestry fragment from the Central or North Coast (Pl. 102).

wearer's rank. They included brightly coloured feathers, animal heads and skins, stuffed birds and pieces of copper or gold in crescent form like the *tumi*, the Indians' ceremonial knife. The artistic activity of this gifted people declined in the eighth century. It has not yet been shown whether rivalry between the various tribal chiefs weakened the Mochica so that they could no longer resist an enemy from outside or whether it was an invasion by the highland Indians that put an end to their culture. But one thing is clear: with the expansion of the Huari culture from the Southern Highlands the independent rule of priests and princes on the North Coast came to an end.

Tiahuanaco-Huari expansion did not encounter an established art style on the Central Coast. This region had produced little of importance before it came under the influence of the great Highland culture. It had always lacked the talent for modelling of the North and the rich palette of the South. Certain textiles are an exception, mostly made of cotton, painted with fantastic scenes and using mineral and organic pigments, but generally speaking we miss the ultimate mastery of technique and the great artistic talent of the imaginative craftsmen of the North and South Coasts. At this period, however, a change took place in the Central Coast region and crafts received new stimuli. The period of the advance of the Tiahuanaco-Huari culture presumably saw the rise of Pachacamac, the sanctuary of a fertility god, in the southern part of the Central Coast. Originally this god was called Iraya; when the Inca established their empire on the coast they called it Pachacamac, and the name was also applied to the sacred place of pilgrimage. In the period of the 'little kingdoms' it was to become a centre for the exchange of ideas and artistic styles along the whole Peruvian coast. The temple-city was also a major burial place. Countless textiles, from the Middle Horizon to the Inca period, have survived here in the desert sands.

For all their supraregional unity these rich finds show a bewildering range of local variations, of transformations of old Tiahuanaco-Huari motifs and elements. The old-established gods and cult forms of the coast made way for new ones from the highlands.

Figs. 61, 62 The 'diagonal double motif', which with the staff-bearer was one of the commonest Middle Horizon patterns, may have originated on textiles (right, from Pl. 91) and then been used in ceramic painting (below, from Pl. 90). A highly stylized bird's wing and a profile head with tearmarks are separated by a diagonal line, and then repeated in alternating form.

The three pattern types characteristic of the Tiahuanaco-Huari style:

Fig.63   The 'composite motif': two highly stylized birds' heads in profile, one light and one dark, are arranged horizontally in such a way that together they form a human face seen in front view (see Pls. 95, 96, 98).

Fig.64   The staff-bearer (see Pls. 86–89).

Fig.65   The diagonal double motif (cp. Pls. 91, 93).

Fig. 66 Another version of the staff-bearer, from a tapestry fragment (Pl. 87).

Even after Tiahuanaco, the religious centre, had lost its extraordinary power to diffuse its arts and ideas and Huari, the secular centre of an enormous area, had lost its political position, this influence remained operative for a long time in textile patterns, though in diluted form and often hard to place chronologically. The now disused Americanist term 'Epigonal Tiahuanaco' was not so far off the mark for this late phase of Tiahuanaco-Huari art, which might indeed be seen as the less distinguished offspring of a notable parent.

Towards the end of the tenth century the original austerity of the style began to relax and the firm adhesion to an established iconography dissolved into a kaleidoscope of capricious local designs. The decorative band in *Plate 107* shows vertically arranged cats with arched back and curled up tail. But if we turn the ingenious pattern on its side the same motifs turn into figures with human features. There is a striking similarity between these anthropomorphized creatures, reproduced as if in motion, and the figures on the decorative band in *Plate 108* which evidently represent priests in cult costume. The Tiahuanacoid influence of the Middle Horizon was exhausted, and the figures from the Gateway of the Sun, which had for so long formed the key image in artistic thought, at last faded away (*Pls. 110, 111*).

In the period that followed the population increased rapidly in parts of the coastal strip, and with the collapse of religious unity separatist currents appeared. Any obstacles to a resurgence of local cultures disappeared. The rise of new 'kingdoms' in the fertile river valleys led to a new form of social life, a new cultural structure and with it a new orientation of art.

Fig. 67 The paintings on Moche ceramics give a meticulous account of costume (see p. 111); paradoxically, textile finds are rare on the North Coast. (After G. Kutscher)

Fig. 68 An overlay interpreting the pattern of the textile reproduced in colour (Pl. 79). After patient analysis, the characteristic staff-bearer can be made out (compare Fig. 54), shown in alternate directions.

79 A textile fragment with highly stylized staff-bearer motifs, which are at first sight hidden among a kaleidoscope of individual symbols and filler elements. The pattern is analysed on the overlay (Fig. 68). South Coast, Tiahuanaco-Huari style, c. 600–800.

79

80 *The Gateway of the Sun at Tiahuanaco, c. 200–600. Its relief patterns are found, in geometricized and abstracted form, on many Middle Horizon textiles (e.g. Figs. 53 and 50–52).*

81–85 *Five vessels displaying features similar to those found on textiles.*

80

83

81

84

82

85

86–88 *Tapestry transformations of the puma-headed staff-bearer on the Gateway of the Sun at Tiahuanaco (cf. Figs. 53, 54) – on a child's tunic or burial robe (opposite; and cp. Fig. 55), on a fragment of tapestry (right; and see Fig. 66), and in decorative bands on a man's garment, where the motif has been completely stylized into an ornament (below; and see Fig. 64). South Coast, Tiahuanaco-Huari style, c. 600–800.*

88

A tapestry fragment showing a design based on the bird-headed staff-bearer on the Gateway of the Sun at Tiahuanaco (Fig. 53). South Coast, Tiahuanaco-Huari style, c.600–800.

90, 91 *Polychrome bowl and tapestry detail displaying the 'diagonal double motif'. In this scheme, completely unlike earlier designs, individual elements such as the divided eye, tear-marks, and bird's wing, appear as symbolic devices in diagonally divided fields (see Figs. 61, 62). South Coast, Tiahuanaco-Huari style, c.600–900.*

Overleaf:

92 *Detail of the puma-headed staff-bearer, reduced to rectangular shapes, from a tapestry band on the robe of a dignitary (see Fig. 56). South Coast, Tiahuanaco-Huari style, c.600–800.*

93, 94 *Tapestry fragments with variations on the diagonal double motif. On the upper one a face in profile alternates with a bird's wing (cp. Pl. 91 and Fig. 65); the lower one consists only of wings. South Coast, Tiahuanaco-Huari style, c.600–900.*

90

93

94

95, 96 *Two details of tapestries showing the composite motif, in which two birds' heads in profile together form a human face (see Fig. 63). South Coast, Tiahuanaco-Huari style, c. 700–900.*

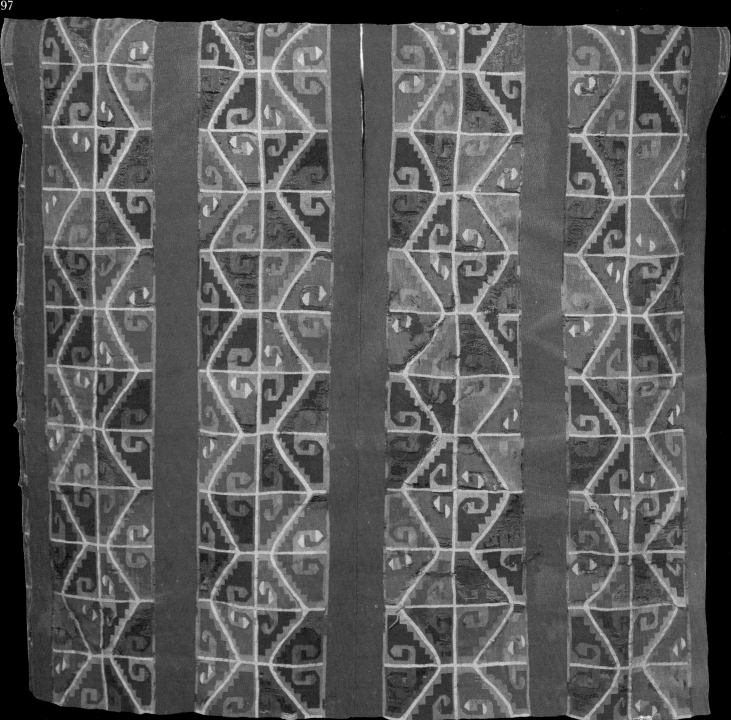

98 *Tapestry fragment with faces formed by the composite motif (see Pls. 95, 96, and Fig. 63), but including hands raised in invocation, a novel element. South Coast, Tiahuanaco-Huari style, c. 700–900.*

99 *Part of a man's garment of tapestry with an as yet uninterpreted subject. The anthropomorphic beings differ from other depictions of the staff-bearer (see Figs. 51–57) chiefly because they appear to be running. South Coast, Tiahuanaco-Huari style, c. 600–1000.*

100, 101 *A double spout and bridge vessel, and a tapestry fragment, on both of which an anthropomorphic figure which is identified as a feline by its fangs has a kind of speech scroll emerging from its mouth. South Coast, Tiahuanaco-Huari style, c.600–900.*

102 *The fragmented rendering of the staff-bearer motif indicates that the weaver of this tapestry was no longer familiar with the classic Tiahuanaco pattern (see the analytical drawing, Fig. 60). Probably Central or North Coast, Tiahuanaco-Huari style, c.700–1000.*

103 *Double-ended snakes with feline heads, and a row of small birds, with a chequer pattern characteristic of the late Tiahuanaco-Huari style. Central Coast (Pachacamac?), c.800–1000.*

100

101

102

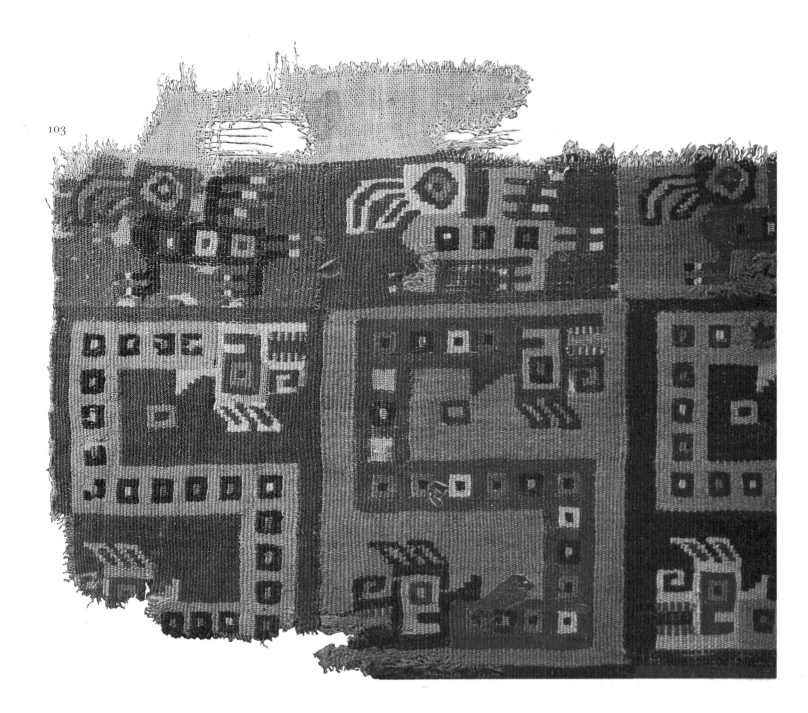

103

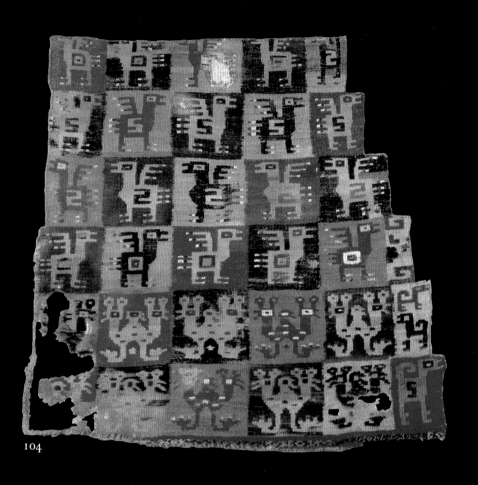

104

104 *Tapestry fragment with birds and other animals. South or Central Coast. Tiahuanaco-Huari style. c. 700–1000.*

105 *Detail of a large tapestry with a pattern made of heads of alternate types, perhaps denoting life and death (see Fig. 59). Probably South Coast. Tiahuanaco-Huari style. c. 600–1000.*

106 *Brocaded textile fragment depicting a semi-feline figure, in a local form by now remote from the original Tiahuanaco staff-bearer (Figs. 50–57). Northern Central Coast. Huarmey. late Tiahuanaco-Huari style. c. 700–1000.*

105

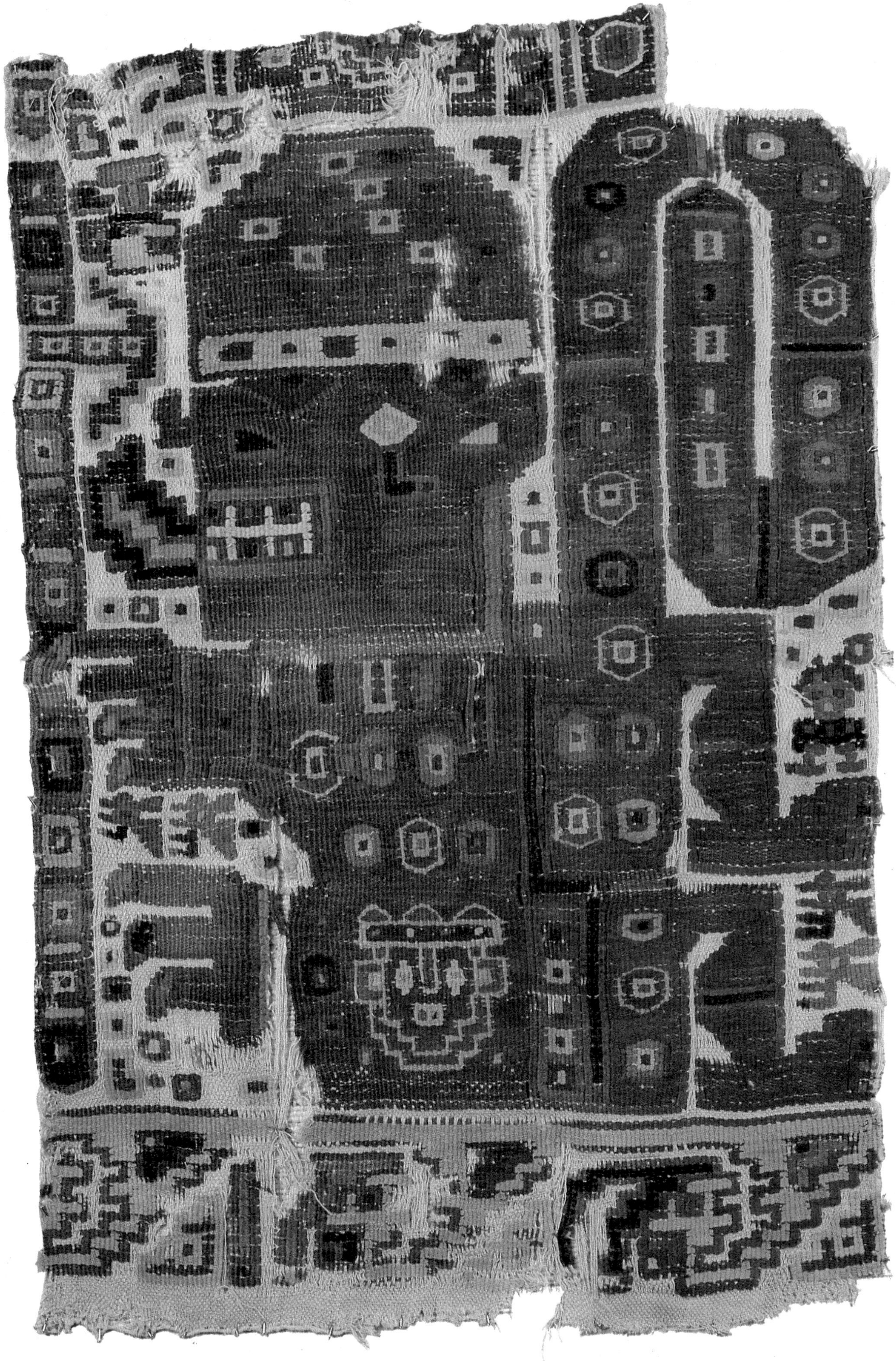

107 *A slit-tapestry hem with an ambiguous motif: looked at as it is printed on the page, it shows vertically superimposed cats with arched backs and curled tails; looked at from the side, their head reveals human features, and their tail suggests a front paw in motion (cp. Pl. 108). Northern Central Coast, Huarmey, Tiahuanaco-Huari style, c.600–900.*

108 *A mythical figure or priest, with zoomorphic features, from an ornamental band. Central Coast (?), late Tiahuanaco-Huari style, c.800–1000.*

109 *Pattern made by the* plangi *tie-dyeing technique (cp. Pl. 78), a device unusual in the Tiahuanaco culture. Southern Highlands, early Tiahuanaco, c.200–800.*

108

109

Overleaf:

110, 111 *Two textile fragments with figures reminiscent of the Staff God on the Gateway of the Sun at Tiahuanaco (Fig. 46), but far removed from the original. Central or North Coast, late Tiahuanaco-Huari style, c. 800–1000.*

112 *Birds of prey on an ornamental band (rep with concealed warp). South Coast (Ica?), late Tiahuanaco-Huari style, c. 800–1000.*

110

111

113

114

113, 114 *Two ornamental bands in slit tapestry, with fish and a parrot-like bird transformed into angular shapes. Northern Central Coast, late Tiahuanaco-Huari style, c.800–1000.*

115–117 *Three headdresses in 'simili-velours' or imitation velvet technique, the first two exhibiting local variants of the staff-bearer motif, and the third llamas accompanied by their young and with an unborn offspring inside them. South Coast, Tiahuanaco-Huari style, c.600–900.*

Overleaf:

118 *A tassel from a shoulder-bag, or part of the ornamental trimming of a garment, embroidered with the figure of a god and a double-headed snake. South or Central Coast, late Tiahuanaco-Huari style, c.800–1000.*

115

116

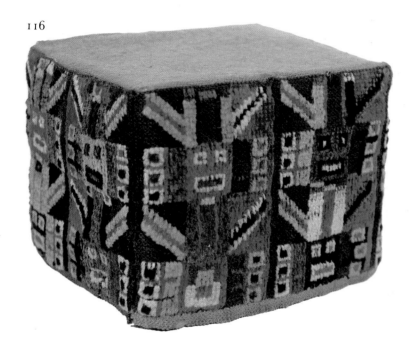

117

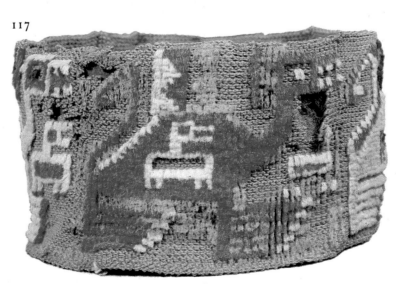

Gods, Spirits, and Beasts

With the fall of Tiahuanaco and Huari (which remains unexplained), the world-picture exported from the highlands to the coast gave way to local traditions. Successful agriculture and skilful use of the land with ever improving irrigation systems led to a population explosion in the coastal region and the foundation of a series of separate and frequently bitterly hostile petty states which the Spanish chroniclers called 'little kingdoms'. The dead were buried almost exclusively in the barren desert strips between the river valleys, so that no valuable agricultural land was wasted. We owe all our knowledge of the prehistoric farming and fishing communities on the edge of the Pacific Ocean to those cemeteries, which were gradually forgotten in remote and (to the living) valueless waste land, and so remained intact for centuries.

In spite of different starting points and developments in the Late Intermediate Period (*c.* 1000–1450), the overall picture of the coastal cultures remained relatively similar. By and large, we no longer find such high intellectual content in textile design, although many masterpieces may have been produced to glorify the rulers. The motifs used by Chimu artists (*Fig. 89; Pls. 150–153*) are the main links with the earlier Mochica mythological concepts. The ancient gods and spirits, Oculate Beings, demons and priests, fertility symbols and sacrificial rites are recorded here and there in textiles, especially on the large painted cotton cloths which presumably decorated the walls of religious buildings. But the spirit which inspired earlier ages, the deep religiosity, the striving to incorporate the whole of a culture's world-picture in textile patterns is no longer pronounced.

In the Late Intermediate Period a more secular manner of representation replaced the supernatural in all the coastal styles. The arrangement in rows and the multiple repetition of attractively stylized zoomorphic and anthropomorphic creatures (*Fig. 90*) obviously suited contemporary taste; even when supernatural beings are depicted they look human rather than divine. The numerous Chancay textiles of the Late Intermediate Period are superbly executed, and their technique, colouring and composition are endlessly rewarding.

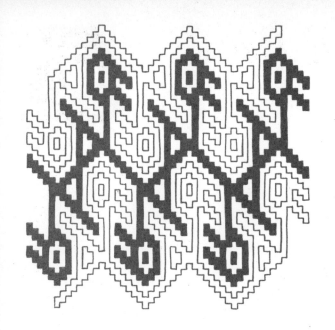

Figs. 69, 70   In the Interlocking style, formalized birds in different colours are repeated head to tail. The arrangement in rows produces a mosaic-like pattern. These examples come from a brocaded border in slit tapestry.

Fig. 71   Double-cloth with a pattern of spotted felines and small birds; in the borders is the stepped meander which in ancient Peru symbolized birds' wings.

The main motifs of this art, which has an underlying unity in spite of an extreme variety in details and colouring that demonstrates the weavers' tireless delight in experimentation, are human figures with hands raised, usually arranged in rows (*Fig. 74; Pls. 163, 164*), and monkey-like creatures, fishes, snakes and frogs (*Pls. 120, 121, 126, 128, 138*). The fierce spotted feline has become a harmless prettified cat (*Fig. 71*). The favourite motif in the Late Intermediate Period seems to have been the bird pattern in the so-called Interlocking style (*Figs. 69, 70*), which was developed on the Central Coast during the Early Intermediate, most probably first in textiles and later in other media. It consists of geometrically stylized animal figures interlocking so skilfully that if you look at the fabric upside down the same pattern appears in another colour. Although this device, which had obviously originated in earlier cultures (e. g. *Pls. 122, 123*), is mainly used with bird motifs, there are also many examples of interlocking snakes, tadpoles, fish and other zoomorphic creatures.

The variety of the figurative repertoire of the period is impressively displayed by pattern bands which seem to have functioned as samplers. These contain many commonly used textile patterns in the smallest possible space. The fabric in *Plate 121* has nine registers, from bottom to top: waves; cats with upright tails; a crablike crustacean, mythological creatures, and realistic and stylized birds; two long-necked birds; smaller stylized birds; two double-headed snakes and tadpole-like creatures; stags and dogs (?) with stylized fish and a bird motif as fillers; and finally two bands of ornament based on birds.

The reason why the religious and mythological motifs and the obscure iconography of the previous millennium's textile patterns gave way to a generally intelligible, more naturalistic imagery is presumably the diminished power of the priestly caste after the collapse of Middle Horizon theocracy. The pilgrimage centre of Pachacamac, already mentioned, played an essential role in the erosion of the differences between individual regional styles in the Late Intermediate Period. To this ancient sanctuary of the fertility

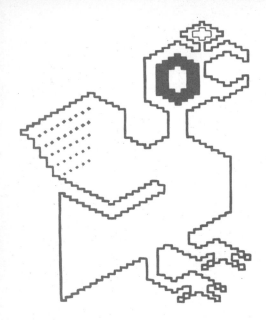

Figs. 72–74   Together with bird motifs, rows of highly stylized human figures with raised hands are one of the most common patterns on textiles in the Late Intermediate Period (cf. Pls. 158, 163, 164).

deity Iraya, founded in the Lurin valley on the Central Coast in the Middle Horizon Period, people came on pilgrimage from all over the country. Their clothing, coca bags and other textiles must have been effective sources of inspiration to the artists. Here offerings from every region streamed in, and different styles met. Thus Pachacamac became an exchange centre for cultures, the melting pot for stylistic movements in process of assimilation. The style, gradually formed along the whole Peruvian coast, was relatively unified, in spite of many variations, and this makes it very difficult for the archaeologist to assign any particular textile of the Late Intermediate Period to a specific region or even a specific local style. The task is made even more difficult by the fact that most of the finds come from grave robberies. It is clear that the rules of religious iconography relaxed, opening the way for hitherto unprecedented transformations and combinations of natural models. The absence of a dominant central figure meant that local variants could multiply indefinitely.

We do not know who the 'lords' of Chavín or Tiahuanaco were, but we can infer something about their view of the universe and get an idea of their pantheon through their art. While the Spanish chroniclers tell us a good deal about the rulers of the 'little kingdoms' on the coast, their accounts give us only a confusing fragmentary picture of the thought and faith of those people. From the archaeological evidence it seems certain that after the decline of the Tiahuanaco-Huari style there was a return to simplicity and clarity of expression (compare *Fig. 3*, from Huaca Prieta, with *Fig. 72*). Yet whereas the potters frequently went over to stereotyped mass-production, often using moulds, many textile products continued to exhibit a high degree of artistry and a remarkable colour sense, even if the patterns lost their complexity and power of expression.

The richest source of textiles from the Late Intermediate Period is the Chancay valley on the Central Coast. Whereas the nearby burial grounds of Ancón and Pachacamac have been extensively plundered by robbers or excavated by archaeologists, those in the Chancay valley, though known for a long time, continue to provide new finds and it is

highly probable that more burial grounds in areas away from the river oases remain to be discovered. Some twenty years ago, when I was working with Peruvian archaeologists on the Central Coast, in a single grave I found more than a dozen bales of strong cotton fabric some 70 cm. wide, wrapped in canvas. The individual cloths, which had a pattern of lengthwise stripes alternately natural colour and dove grey, were between 12 and 20 m. long – all in the grave of a single man. Were they the personal possessions of some high dignitary, or a weaver's stock placed in the grave with him? It was impossible to say. Since the patterns were of little artistic interest, samples were taken for the museum and the rest of the cloth was given to the site workers, who sold it in Lima as covers for deckchairs and garden chairs – about a thousand years after it was woven! What better evidence could there be for the Chancay weavers' standards of craftsmanship?

Politically the Chancay region formed part of the Cuismancu kingdom, as the Spanish-Inca chronicler Garcilaso de la Vega called it. This was a confederation of small regional states whose sphere of influence stretched from the southern border of the Chimu kingdom to the Lurin valley south of Lima. We can gain little knowledge of the imaginative life of this territory in the Late Intermediate Period from its ceramics, which are limited to a handful of expressionless standard types, as though the artistic and technical experience of the potters of the previous two thousand years had been forgotten. The awkwardly proportioned vessels are more like the naive efforts of children working with plasticine than the products of craftsmen, and mass-production apparently forced the potters to simplify their decoration. Painting, mainly with geometric motifs, is done in dull black and violet-grey with an occasional patch of matt red.

The situation is very different when we come to Chancay textiles, which include most of the pattern bands found to date (*Pls. 121, 126, 147*). The weavers had mastered nearly every technique of weaving and decoration then known, from double-cloth to superbly worked, astonishingly fine openwork gauze with knotted-in patterns (*Pls. 22, 119, 124*), tapestry, brocade, *plangi* and *ikat* tie-dyeing (a speciality of the Chancay weavers), and

Fig. 75   Human figures, from
a double-cloth.

Fig. 76   Two llamas depicted
in slit tapestry.

positive painting. Indeed, a single fabric frequently combines several techniques (*Pl. 163*). The remarkable gauzes mostly consist of overtwisted cotton yarn and were made by using a frame completely covered with 'scaffold' wefts which could be removed later; the intermittent weaves, in which the warp threads as well as the weft travel only over specific stretches of the net construction, were only produced in ancient Peru. These gauzes, mainly used as scarves, exhibit a wide variety of simple but impressive patterns produced by attaching, knotting and twining additional threads onto the net stretched on the frame.

Another peculiarity of Chancay textile art is the large, frequently square, painted cotton cloths, many in brilliant orange and various shades of brown, some even in a special turquoise blue that is extremely rare in Peruvian textiles. The colours are also very boldly contrasted in the tapestries and slit tapestries, and their variety makes up for the repetitive disposition of the motifs, among which wild cats, monkey-like creatures, fish and birds are commonest. The weaver's imagination also produced figures for which there was no model in nature. *Plate 131*, for example, shows creatures which look like birds with a red deer's antlers. The wide range of possibilities available to textile artists in the Late Intermediate Period not only stimulated their imagination in the invention of anthropomorphic, zoomorphic and fabulous creatures, it also allowed them to experiment with the combination of the most varied techniques in a single garment and was one of the factors leading to the revival of wool embroidery.

At the same time we find a design formula rare in Peru – a predilection for flat patches of undifferentiated colour. The effect depends essentially on either a harmony or a tension between specific shades. The possible permutations were endless and were exploited enthusiastically by the Chancay weavers, who had no scruples about disregarding all the rules of symmetry and balance. An interesting example of this is the pattern on a painted cotton fabric (*Fig. 78*): this uses various shades of brown, sometimes as simple outline and sometimes with lighter internal drawing, to show stylized human figures,

147

Fig. 77   A tadpole, symbol of
fertility, from a decorative
border.

Fig. 78   Part of a Chancay
painted cotton cloth displays a
'dancer', birds, and interlocking stylized fish. The drawing
looks almost childlike, but the
composition is varied and
original.

birds and fish in square fields. Some squares contain only one figure, while others have horizontal 'friezes' and interlocking diagonally arranged animal motifs. The patterns repeat, but in different colours.

South of Chancay lie the Chincha and Ica valleys. The valleys of the South Coast of Peru are narrower than those of the Central and Northern Coasts, and the states established in them were scarcely big enough to be considered as 'kingdoms'; although 'kings' are frequently mentioned in Spanish accounts of this period, it would be more accurate to think of them as tribal lords. There are very slight reminiscences in the Ica style of the great tradition of Nazca textile art, which had its centre a little further south some five hundred years earlier. Typical Ica textile patterns are recorded on ceramic vessels (*Pls. 148, 149*). It is possible, however, to point to textiles found at South Coast sites which on stylistic grounds alone might well be called Nazca: such are a sleeveless garment with two felines as the main decoration and interlocking birds in the border (*Pl. 125*), and a fragment of slit tapestry displaying highly stylized human figures wearing peculiar headdresses (*Pl. 158*). Imported goods, or adaptation? I favour the latter.

Chronicles from the period of the Spanish conquest tell us something about the Chincha state and to some extent explain historical connections and social development in other Peruvian coastal regions of the Late Intermediate Period. According to these accounts the basic economic and social unit was the clan. The clan owned the cultivable land, which was divided among its members. Families managed it largely as private property, though they were not allowed to dispose of it or bequeath it outside the clan. Within, it could be left to the son who 'seemed to be the worthiest'. The mass of the population was divided into the 'free' men, who were liable to taxation, and the 'unfree', probably delinquents and prisoners of war, who lived a life of slavery. The chieftains exercised authority over every aspect of daily life. When a wedding took place the chief of the tribe to which the bride belonged received part of the bride price, of which the rest went to the bride's family. This consisted of llamas and valuable objects such as

149

Fig. 79 Hybrid zoomorphic creatures on a slit tapestry.

Fig. 80 A Chimu textile showing a high-ranking warrior, wearing the sickle-shaped headdress typical of North Coast dignitaries. He holds a weapon in one hand and in the other the severed head of an enemy.

clothes and textiles, the amount calculated according to the bridegroom's means.

If the term 'feudal kingdom' can properly be applied to any of the small states of Peru, it certainly can to Chimu on the North Coast, already mentioned at the beginning of this chapter. This state extended from Tumbes in the north to Paramonga in the south, and between 1000 and 1460, when it too was swallowed by the Incas' advance, was the biggest and most important state on the Peruvian coast. Its culture stemmed from that of the Moche, but Chimu works of art seldom achieved the realism and originality of their predecessors. One legacy of Moche art is the worldly character of all representations, even when they have a symbolic meaning; another appears in specific details, such as the headdress shaped like a *tumi* (*Fig. 80*). But Chimu art is on the whole less accomplished and less varied in its motifs, failings that are particularly apparent in ceramics. The expressive vase painting of the Mochica, from which their way of life, clothing, jewellery and even body painting is placed vividly before our eyes, often down to the smallest detail (*Figs. 5, 67*), is replaced by a coarse decoration that is frequently impressed rather than painted. Chimu textiles, however, delight the eye with their brilliant colours and appealing small stylized animal figures (*Fig. 73*). As in the subsequent Inca period, the Chimu dignitaries and head of state wore magnificent robes. A detailed account of the life of the Peruvian coastal Indians written by the Spaniard Miguel Cabello de Balboa between 1576 and 1586 mentions a legendary 'mighty ruler' in the valley of Lambayeque (north of Chanchan) called Naymlap, whose servants included a craftsman who 'was entrusted with the production of robes and precious feather clothing'.[14]

There is a striking similarity between Chimu textile patterns (*Figs. 81–87*) and the relief decoration, formerly plastered and painted, on the walls of the buildings of the Chimu capital, Chanchan (*Pls. 144, 145*). This city, with up to 250,000 inhabitants in an area of 18 square kilometres, divided into ten walled precincts, was the most densely populated in Peru in the period of the 'little kingdoms'. The decorative motifs cut into

151

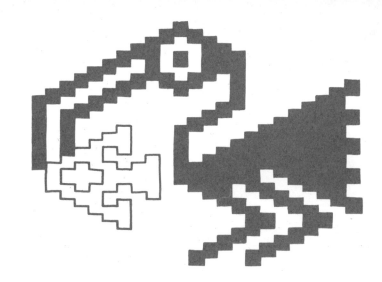

Figs. 81–87 Sea birds and parrots inspired the weavers of the Late Intermediate Period to create their most appealing textile patterns. They appear in both naturalistic and stylized form on clothes and burial cloths. The same motifs are also found on ceramics and on the palace walls of Chanchan (Pls. 144, 145).

its massive walls when the *adobe* was still moist are of a simple (one might almost say trivial) nature, and they are evenly distributed over the surface – features characteristic of Chimu art in general.

There is a similar correspondence between the scenes populated with many figures that appear in relief on the sides of the pyramid known as the Huaca del Dragón, outside Chanchan (*Pl. 146*), and those on large painted cotton fabrics from the North Coast; naive and completely individual in their drawing and brilliant in their colouring, these designs reflect ancient beliefs. One of these cloths, for instance, which was probably part of a large wall-hanging (*Pl. 151*), shows a mythological scene in attractively natural terms: a naked human figure with the soles of his feet turned towards us stands beneath the double-headed jagged snake, symbol of the firmament. In his left hand he holds an object which can be interpreted as a sceptre, rattle or club. A *tumi* lies on the ground to his right. Perhaps the coloured circles and triangles are supposed to represent the starry sky and the upside-down human face surrounded by spikes (rays?), on the upper right, the sun sinking into the Pacific. The sign below this, reminiscent of a starfish, might be a symbol of the waxing and waning moon.

Little is known about the Chimu religion, but the Spanish chroniclers stated with certainty that this people paid particular honour to the moon, the star of the night whose dew was required for the fields to prosper, as opposed to the all-consuming sun. In his book *Corónica moralizada del orden de San Augustín en el Peru* (Barcelona 1638), Antonio de la Calancha relates what the Indians of the north coastal region, with whom he lived for years on friendly terms, told him about the moon:[15]

the Indians of Pacasmayo and the other valleys of the coast worshipped the moon as the supreme deity. For they believed it held sway over all the elements, caused the fruits of the earth to grow, roused the turbulence of the sea and called up thunder and lightning . . . They believed it mightier than the sun, which does not shine at night, whereas the moon can be seen by day as well as by night. Another reason was that the moon often darkened the sun, but the sun never overshadowed the moon . . . At eclipses of the sun they used to hold feasts in honour of the moon's victory over the sun.

154

Fig. 88 Detail of a Chimu painted cotton cloth depicting monkeys and parrots in square fields.

Fig. 89 A highly stylized animal, perhaps a llama, on a border in Chancay style.

A similar mythological scene appears on another wall-hanging fragment (*Pl. 152*). Here there is a stylized fish above the bent arm on the right and a puma head on the far left. The recurrent stepped motif can no longer be interpreted simply as bird's feathers (as in Tiahuanaco-Huari designs); what significance it may have had is now lost. Striking signs of rank, in addition to the *tumi*-shaped headdress, are the large earplugs, which were also common in the Inca period and led the Spaniards to call Indian dignitaries *orejones* ('big ears'). This figure too stands below a jagged snake symbolizing the firmament.

Junius Bird produced firm evidence to indicate that fabrics of this kind were wall-hangings for religious buildings. For years he collected photographs and drawings of examples in different collections and compared their size, motifs and styles, testing the possibility that several of them might actually belong together. The result showed that many of them actually fitted perfectly together, proving that these magnificent textiles had been deliberately cut up by grave robbers and sold all over the world as fragments. For example, Bird managed to track down twelve pieces similar to the fragment reproduced in *Plate 153*, which measures about 185×175 cm., and, although seven sections still cannot be found, he was able to reconstruct the original sequence of picture stories for a complete wall-hanging more than 32 m. long. The central field of the panel illustrated shows prisoners with ropes around their necks or bodies, and between them other naked figures, birds of prey and the double-headed snake, familiar from the earliest times. The central figure is obviously the victor. Four trophy heads in the lower area indicate that a cult ceremony, presumably connected with the sacrifice of the captured warriors, is represented.

This scene can be paralleled on an item of clothing which presumably belonged to a priest (*Pl. 165*). Here, on a coarse plain weave ground decorated with wool brocading and 'appliqué' borders, are embroidered motifs of double-headed snakes, sea birds and human figures who, as the rope around their neck indicates, are surely prisoners.

Fig. 90 A mysterious slit tapestry motif which might be interpreted as a fish or as a marine deity important to the fish-eating coastal Indians (cp. also *Fig. 15*).

119 Detail of an openwork gauze fabric incorporating stylized demons' heads or Oculate Beings. Chancay or Ancón, c. 1000–1400.

The Chimu were undoubtedly the most powerful opponents of the Inca, who from about 1438 began their rapid rise to supreme power. The 'coastal kingdom' must have seemed impregnable, with its troops trained in many wars of conquest and its borders protected by numerous fortifications. But it fell, the last of the 'little kingdoms', into the hands of the Inca in 1461 and became part of their empire. One result was the imposition of an art style in which there was almost no figurative representation. Yet the old symbols were not completely eradicated on the coast. The hybrid creature shown in *Figure 90*, from a slit tapestry, might be interpreted in many ways – as swimming fish, or flying bird, or the Oculate Being, or a marine deity of the coast dwellers who survived mainly on fish (see also *Pls. 127, 164, 166*). As before we are amazed by the feeling for colour and the perfect craftsmanship of the weavers, whose skill also opened the way to all kinds of new forms for the emphatically geometric style of ornament that came to the fore under the Inca.

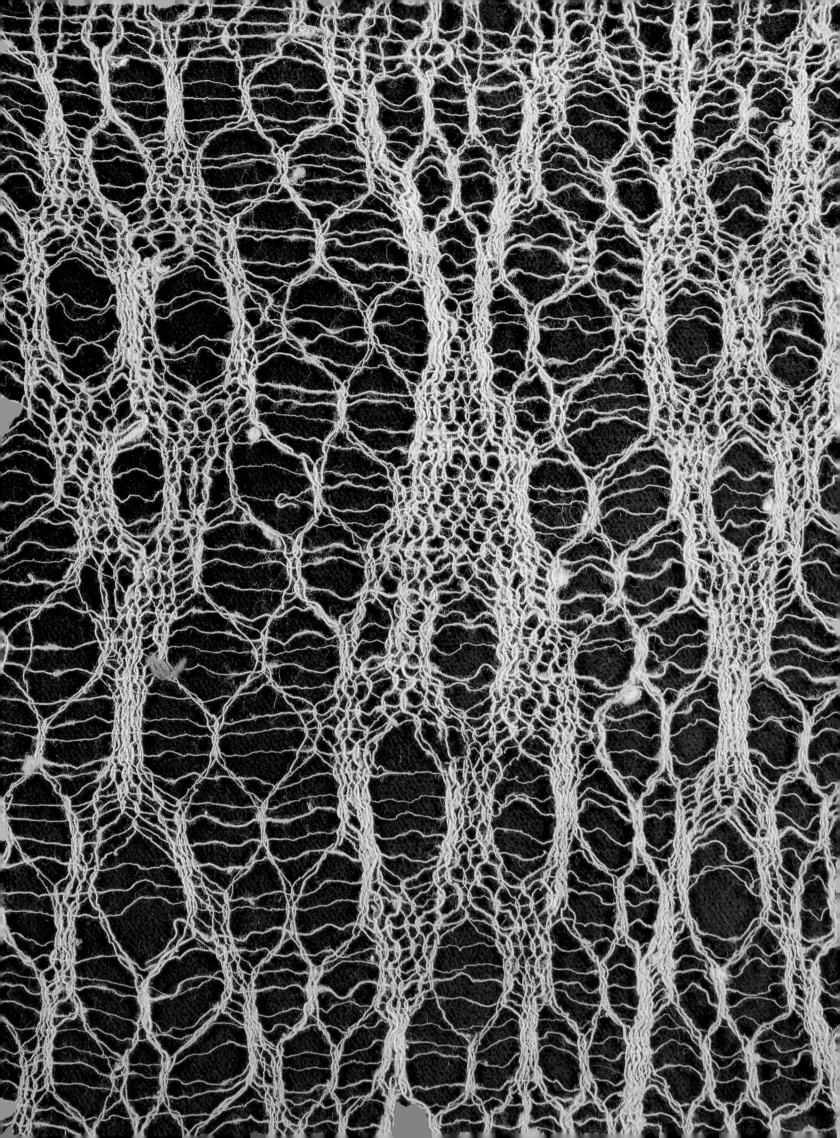

120 *Monkey-like figure on a brocaded fabric; the upper and lower borders are woven in tapestry technique. Chancay, c. 1000–1200.*

121 *Tapestry pattern band displaying a number of commonly used motifs. Chancay, c. 1000–1400.*

120

121

122–124 *Geometrically
stylized interlocking snakes, on
a stirrup-spout vessel (Moche,
c. AD 100–600), in adobe
decoration (from the pyramid of
Licapa in the Chicama valley,
c. 300 BC–AD 300), and in an
openwork gauze (Chancay,
c. 1000–1400).*

122

123

124

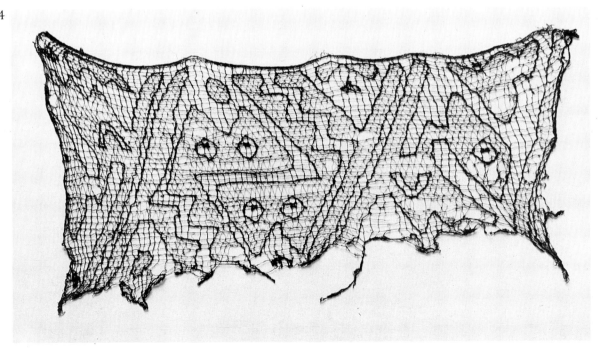

125

125 *Garment with two felines on the body and highly stylized birds in interlocking style on the border. Ica, c. 1000–1400.*

126 *The great variety of demons and other motifs brocaded on this plain weave cloth suggests a sampler. Chancay, c. 1000–1400.*

126

127 *Sea bird holding a fish (cp. Fig. 90); this central brocaded motif is framed by bands which incorporate tiny birds. Central or South Coast, c. 1000–1400.*

128, 129 *Frogs or toads as a motif for embroidery and carved out of mother-of-pearl. Central or South Coast, c. 1000–1400.*

130 *Cats, on a brocaded fabric. Chancay, c. 1000–1400.*

131 *Stag-like creatures, on a brocaded fabric. Chancay, c. 1000–1400.*

132 *Birds holding trophy heads in their beaks, on a brocaded fabric. Pachacamac, c. 1000–1400.*

132

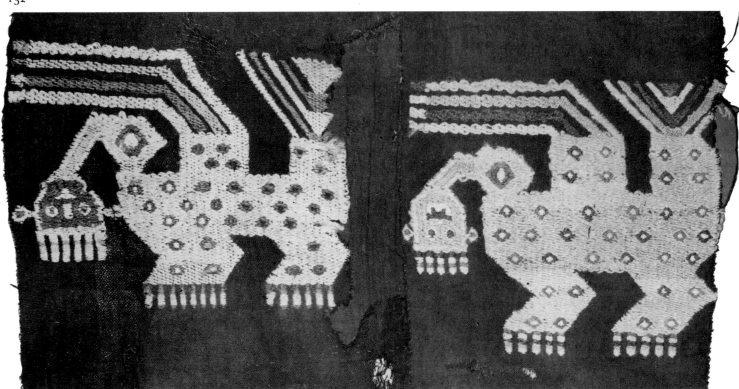

133

134

133 *A brocaded fragment incorporating the ancient motif of a bird within a bird; in the border, interlocking birds. North Coast, c. 1000–1400.*

134 *A pattern formed of identical bird motifs embroidered in different colours. Central Coast, c. 1000–1400.*

135 *A lively, if coarsely worked, embroidered bird. Chancay, c. 1000–1400 or earlier.*

135

136

137

138

136, 137 *Interlocking birds painted by stencil – one way of permitting a kind of mass-production of decorated fabrics (others were printing by cylinder or flat stamp). Central and North Coast, c. 1000–1400.*

138 *Sea birds and interlocking fish or snakes painted in alternate stripes. Central Coast (?), c. 1000–1400.*

139 *Slit tapestry garment, with rows of birds facing in opposite directions as the central pattern, and ornamental borders with an interlocking bird motif sewn on at top and bottom. The plain triangle with a woven 'false border' simulates a neck opening. Chimu (?). c. 1000–1400.*

140 *A border with woven fringe; the pattern of paired birds is worked in slit tapestry with additional brocading threads. North or Central Coast, c. 1000–1400.*

140

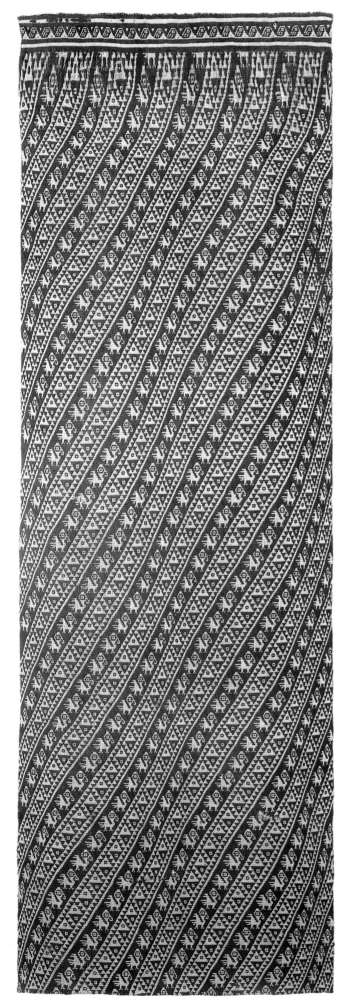

141

141 *Long cotton fabric, probably part of a wall-hanging, with birds and geometric ornaments in diagonal stripes. Central Coast, c. 1300–1450.*

142 *Two richly ornamented robe hems. In the upper one, basic slit tapestry is supplemented by embroidery and applied slit tapestry decorations, and the cords and tassels take the form of plant and blossom symbols. In the lower one, diagonal bands of zigzags and interlocking birds are outlined by an openwork mesh background. North and Central Coast, Early Chimu and Chimu style, c. 1000–1400.*

143 *Detail of a painted cotton fabric using interlocking birds in a wavy rather than angular form. Chancay (?), c. 1000–1400.*

142

144

144, 145 *Details of the relief decoration in adobe at the ruined city of Chanchan. The motifs were originally plastered and painted in colours, increasing their already strong resemblance to textile patterns (cp. Pls. 121, 138, and Fig. 84). Chimu, c. 1200–1450.*

146 *Detail of the Huaca del Dragón near Chanchan. The iconographical motifs appear in similar form on painted textiles (e.g. Pl. 153). Chimu, c. 1200–1450.*

145

147

148

149

147 *Commonly used motifs on a double-cloth pattern band. Chancay, c. 1000–1400.*

148, 149 *Bowls with painted polychrome decoration of the kind that also characterizes Ica textiles. South Coast, c. 1000–1450.*

150 *Fragments of a painted cotton textile depicting fishermen or warriors in boats. Chimu (?), c. 1000–1400.*

151   151

152

151 *Painted cotton textile, probably part of a large wall-hanging, with a wealth of symbolic features. A naked human figure holding a cere-monial staff and* tumi *stands below a double-headed jagged snake representing the firma-ment (see p. 153). North Coast, perhaps from Huarmey, c. 1000–1400.*

152 *Another painted fragment showing the double-headed jagged snake. The human fig-ure's prominent earplugs are carefully depicted (see p. 155). Chimu, c. 1000–1250.*

153 *A painted fabric which has been shown to be part of a wall-hanging some 32 m long. It shows a religious ceremony, probably connected with the sacrifice of captured warriors, who are depicted with ropes round their necks and waists (cp. Pl. 146, and see p. 155). Chimu (?), c. 1000–1250.*

154

154 *Brocaded motif with interlocking birds. Central or North Coast, c. 1000–1400.*

155, 156 *The central figure in these two slit tapestry panels is a richly clad god or priest, flanked by four birds. Chancay, c. 1000–1400.*

155

157

157 *Brocaded fragment with fringed borders at top and bottom. Central North Coast, c. 1000–1400.*

158 *Fragment of slit tapestry showing human figures with their hands raised. Ica valley, c. 1000–1400.*

159 *Fragment of double-cloth with stylized monsters. North Coast (?), c. 1000–1450.*

160 *Double-cloth fragment where the bird motif has become part of an ornamental pattern. North Coast (?), c. 1000–1450.*

159

158

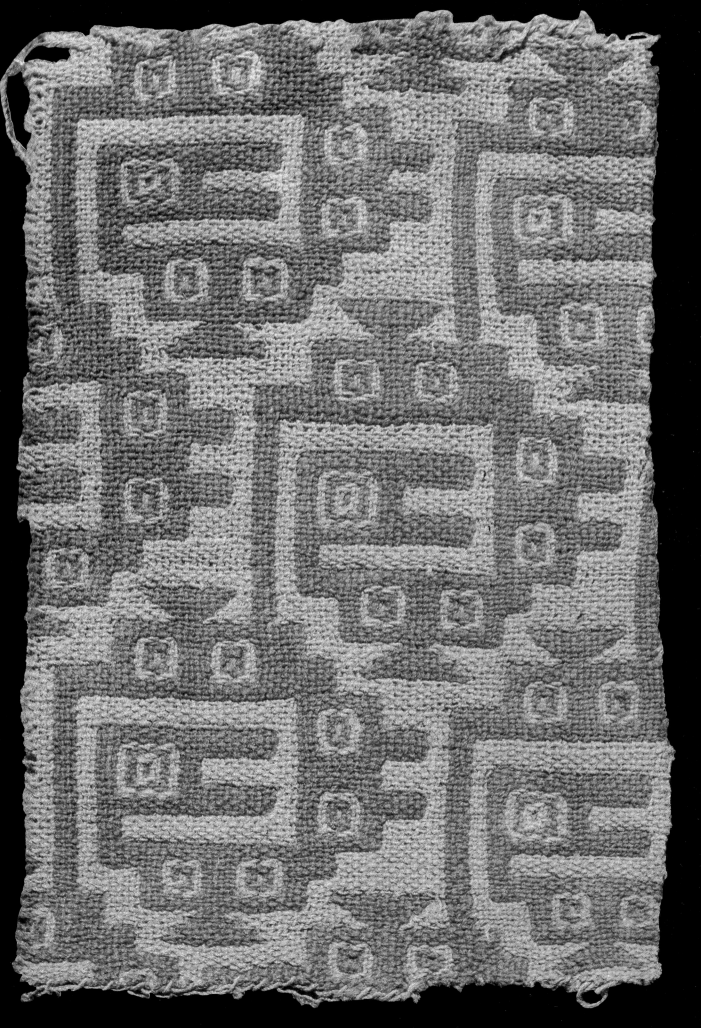

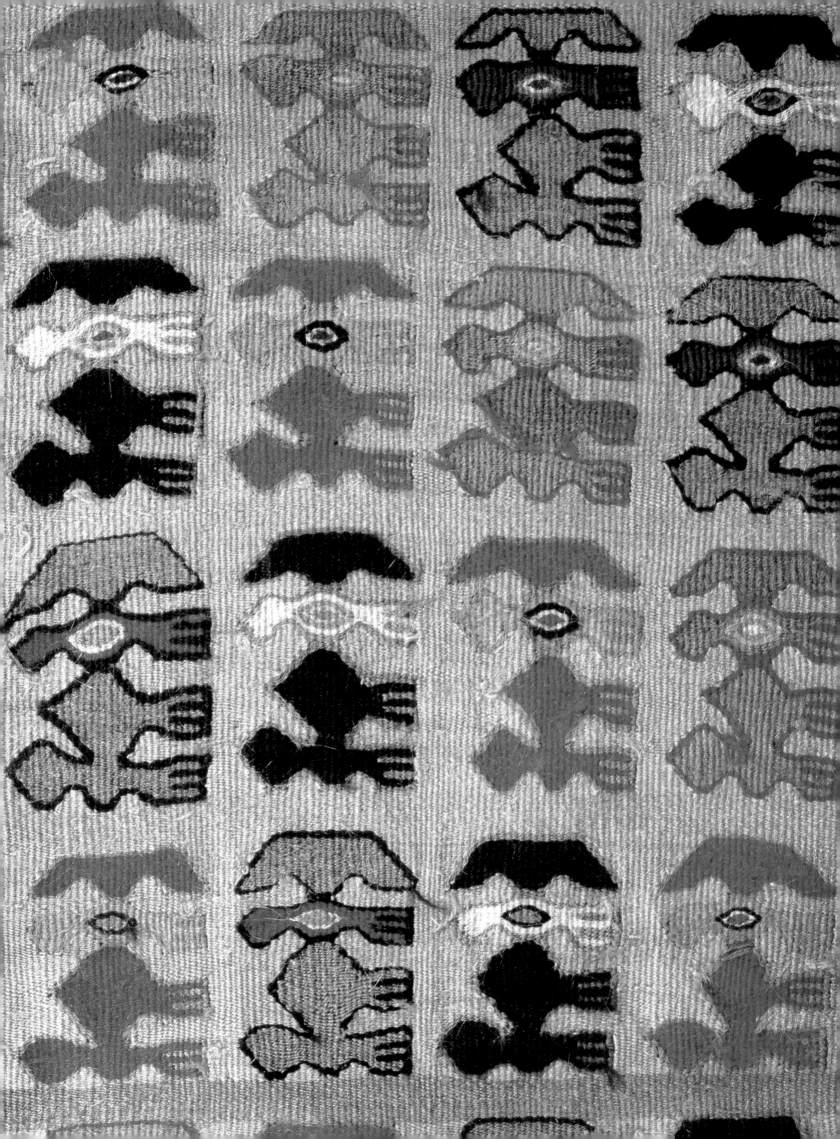

161 *Stags with stylized antlers in the form of a sickle-shaped headdress, in slit tapestry. North or Central Coast, c. 1000–1400.*

162 *Three ornamental tassels in slit tapestry, probably part of a ceremonial robe. Chancay, c. 1000–1400.*

163 *One of a row of figures wearing sickle-shaped head-dresses, from a slit tapestry border. Chancay or Chimu. c. 1000–1400.*

164 *Fragment of a man's garment in slit tapestry with humans wearing sickle-shaped headdresses, interspersed with fish. Chimu. c. 1100–1400.*

163

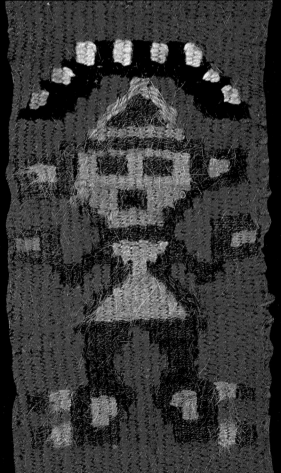

164

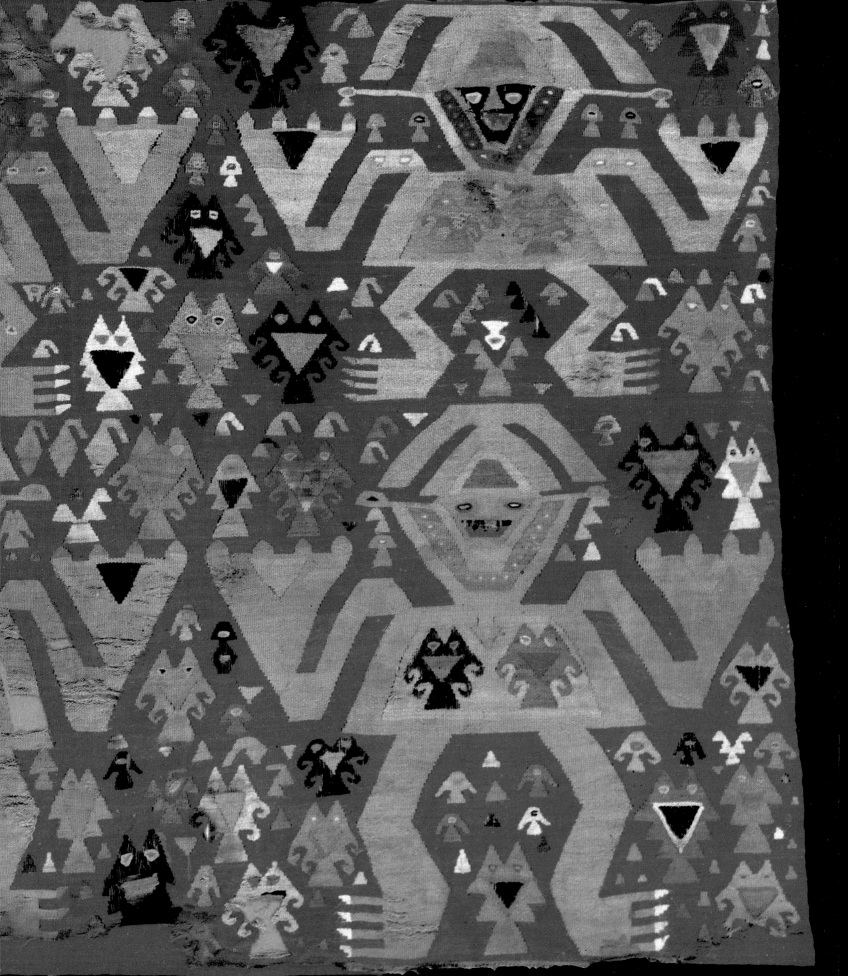

165 *Shirt with embroidered motifs including men with ropes round their necks (prisoners?) and zoomorphic creatures. Chimu, c. 1000–1400.*

165

The Inca Empire

The Inca style finds its purest and most incisive expression in textile art. There are no direct models for it in ancient Peru. The break comes imperceptibly, with a gradual abandonment of the visual language of earlier Indian cultures. Geometric ornament, the division of the surface into rectangles, stripes and other geometric forms, now becomes all-pervasive. Mythical creatures almost cease to exist as motifs.

The Inca state was one of the largest and most interesting power-structures in world history. With the help of a strong military force and a rigidly organized hierarchy of officials, a relatively small élite was able to impose its rule from present-day Ecuador to Peru, Bolivia, north-west Argentina and northern Chile. It is not surprising, therefore, that the whole idea of the ancient Indian civilization in South America is associated in the popular mind with the romantic name of the 'Inca Empire'. Yet the Inca were only the heirs to a development going back three thousand years. The great empire itself lasted less than a hundred years and its culture was based on the achievements of countless conquered Indian peoples and several earlier cultures. This fact was deliberately ignored by the official Inca 'historiography', and most of the chroniclers who came to Peru after the Spanish conquest did not have the evidence to assess the situation more accurately, although some genuine and valuable attempts to collect material about pre-Inca history were made.[16] In any case, folk memories at the time of the conquest probably went no further back than three or four generations at most, i.e. little more than a century. So inevitably it is to the surviving artefacts that we have to turn for the main source of information about the achievements of earlier periods. Even for the Inca period we know that what has survived is only a fraction of what once existed. Some of the Europeans who came into contact with Indians and their art left accounts of the massive Inca buildings. They wrote about the 'god king' Sapa Inca[17] and his magnificent household unmatched by any European ruler. And they wrote about the splendid highways with rest-houses and stores which facilitated the Spaniards' advance and had no equivalent in Europe. These writings are also our only source of information on the great campaigns of conquest undertaken by the Inca army.

Figs. 91, 92 Illustrations from the chronicle of Huaman Poma de Ayala showing the Inca's sister-wife (left), and the Inca himself borne in a litter with his sister-wife and his heir.

'Inca' does not mean a tribe, but a dynasty, at whose head stood the revered Inca lord as 'Son of the Sun'. The role assigned to the 'Children of the Sun' as bringers of culture is emphasized in the saga of the divine origin of the first Inca. Garcilaso de la Vega, himself half-Inca, recorded it in his *Comentarios reales:*

Thou knowest that in ancient times all this land was desolate and bare and the people lived like wild beasts, without civilization. When our Father, the Sun God, saw this, he had compassion and sent down from heaven one of his sons, Manco Capac, and a daughter, Mama Ocllo, so that the people should recognize him as God and learn how to live reasonably and peacefully together . . . Then the first Inca said to his wife and sister: 'Let us settle here to fulfil our Father's wish.' They gathered many people round them and instructed them in all activities and arts. Manco Capac taught the men, and his sister-wife, the Queen, taught the women weaving and other arts . . .

To millions of Indians the Inca was not only the highest political and religious authority of the state, but also a god on earth. The common man never saw his face and even the Inca's closest relatives and the highest officers of the state had to remove their sandals before him and carry a symbolic burden on their shoulders, so that they should always be conscious of the gulf that lay between them and the God King. How could a mere artist, a subject, ever dare to depict him? The result was that the repertoire of imagery was exhausted in ceramics, in architecture, in sculpture and in metalwork. Textile patterns were the hardest hit of all. As the plates show, the teeming world of gods, priests, warriors, and animals gives way in this last phase of ancient Indian artistic creativity to bare abstract ornament (*Pls. 167, 174*).

The reasons why artists chose to use abstraction as a means of expression in the art of earlier cultures has already been mentioned. The artists of Chavín and Paracas, Nazca and Tiahuanaco were in many ways trying to do the same thing as Surrealist painters in our own century. They placed several creatures or even parts of these creatures (eyes, mouth, wings, etc.) next to each other or imperceptibly merged them together. What they achieved was a sort of 'fourth dimension' – an ability to see existence simultaneously at several levels. Demarcations are abolished by overlapping; many-layered

superimpositions endow the image with multiple meanings, a deeper significance that lies at the heart of all these hybrid monsters of earlier cultures. The feline conquered the air when it was given wings, and the realm of water when it had fish attributes. Although this kind of abstraction goes far beyond real models the individual elements of it do exist in nature. The diagonal double motif (*Figs. 61, 62, 65*), for instance, may ultimately be an attempt to turn cosmic processes into an impressive image, or, in other words, to give visible expression to something that was invisible, and many-layered. This explains both the broad range of individual variations within ancient Indian art and also its fidelity to certain basic motifs found in all textiles – from Chavín, the first great culture, to the period of the 'little kingdoms'.

The abstraction of Inca art is of a different kind. What we find here is the absolute predominance of linear geometric form, to the exclusion of anything organic. The decoration of the cloths, the wall-hangings in the great palaces of the rulers (every Inca had his own palace) and the patterns on the many sumptuous robes of the dignitaries, all obey this principle. There is something repellent about its rigidity and the static nature of the geometric design. Perhaps this was intentional. The stark, clear ornaments may have been meant to express an aura of ceremonial solemnity, of aloofness surrounding the wearer, an effect not easy to achieve in clothes decorated with the tiny, elaborate, overcrowded patterns of, for instance, the tribal chiefs of Chancay. In Inca ceramics, too, figurative forms make only a fleeting appearance, for instance in the shape of the handles of shallow clay bowls (*Figs. 93, 95*). Examples such as the sketchily modelled puma head on an aryballoid jar of light-coloured clay (*Pl. 168*) are unexciting compared with the classical beauty of the form and the painting – the simple but fascinating herringbone pattern and the equally typical Inca line-and-cross motif integrated into rhythmically arranged bands.

There are isolated figurative motifs on fabrics: on a slit tapestry (*Pl. 166*) we find stylized creatures in which we can recognize the ancient fish deities that were common

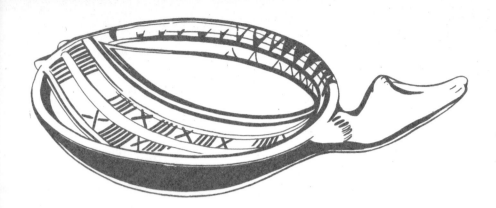

textile motifs in earlier times on the coast. Similarly ancient bird motifs occur in horizontal and vertical bands on a large cloth (*Pl. 175*). The geometrically stylized human face on a slit tapestry (*Fig. 105*) also looks back to the earlier tradition. Often typical Inca motifs blend with these ancient patterns, as for example in a textile fragment on which the Inca flower – the serrated clubhead, also called the 'morning star' motif – stands next to depictions of birds (*Pl. 170*). Such textile patterns are in a sense the tribute paid by the victors to the vanquished. But they are not characteristic of the Inca period. Its style is marked by a clear-cut end to the expression of individuality in art. Unification was not just a political programme: it was an artistic one too. Standardized rational thought becomes the basis of most handicrafts. As a result the repertoire of textile patterns surviving from the Inca period is very limited.

From sixteenth- and seventeenth-century written and illustrated sources we have a fairly accurate idea of the clothing worn in the Inca Empire. The illustrations and explanations in Huaman Poma de Ayala's chronicle (*Nueva Corónica y Buen Gobierno*) are particularly interesting. Huaman Poma came from a distinguished Inca family. The Spaniards christened him Felipe. He learnt the language of the conquerors, and presumably also how to read and write, in a school run by a religious order. For many years he worked on a chronicle the primary intention of which was to draw the attention of the Spanish throne to the despotism of colonial administration and the injustice reigning in Peru. He completed his work in 1587, and in 1613 it was mentioned as being in the possession of the King of Spain. Then this invaluable original Indian document was mislaid for centuries, until 1908, when Richard Pietschmann discovered it in the Royal Library at Copenhagen.

Neither the time lag of a few decades between the end of the Inca period and the compilation of his chronicle nor the fact that Huaman Poma had been taught by Spanish missionaries diminishes the value of his work, which includes several hundred drawings, clumsy and naive, but all the more interesting for that very reason. The

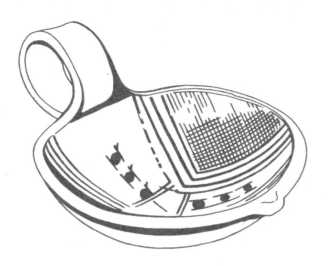
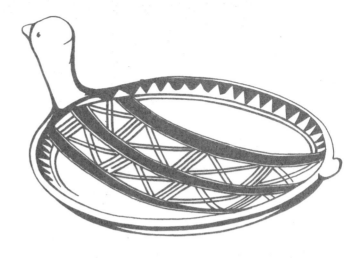

key fact about his chronicle is that it is the work of a Quechua Indian who was in close contact with the customs and usages, ideas and mentality of his fellow countrymen. The garments in his drawings correspond very closely to the textiles of this and earlier ages excavated from graves by archaeologists. Huaman Poma de Ayala's natural understanding of the world of his fathers and his eye for the essential make his chronicle an inexhaustible source for students of Inca culture. He illustrates the common hand spindle, being used by a hunchbacked woman (*Fig. 99*) and by a young girl (*Fig. 104*), and shows the posture of a woman at the belt loom (*Fig. 101*). We learn a great deal about the typical clothing and textiles at the Inca court, for example in a drawing in which the sister-wife of the Inca is shown with her maids (*Fig. 91*), where even the ornamental pins with which the cloaks were held together are visible. This detail appears even more clearly in a drawing of an Indian noblewoman (*Fig. 103*).

A striking feature of some drawings (*Figs. 92, 96*) is a strange clothing pattern consisting of repeated signs. The recurring '4' is surely attributable to the chronicler's European upbringing, but other signs, arranged in a chequerboard pattern, seem to lend weight to the theory that the Indians had a genuine script. The Spanish chronicler Cieza de León, writing in 1541,[18] mentions the *quipu*, a set of knotted strings (*Fig. 97*) used by the Incas to record the vast quantities of conquered property and the rate of tribute to be levied. Cieza de León learnt that 'the knots stood for the numbers 1–10, 10–100 and 100–1,000' and that the different colours of the woollen strings, as well as their arrangement and the arrangement of the knots, had a specific meaning. Quantities were indicated by a system of knots based on the decimal system, and the colour of the string stood for the object being counted. Every Inca governor was allotted an interpreter trained in deciphering this kind of record. In one of his drawings Huaman Poma de Ayala shows a *quipu* interpreter (*Fig. 98*), with an Inca abacus in the lower left corner. But although a great deal of information may have been expressed by using the different combinations of colour, grouping and sequence of knots and strings, it was definitely

Fig. 96 The Inca Viracocha, from the chronicle of Huaman Poma de Ayala. His robe has a pattern made up of repeated signs in squares.

not a script. The *quipu* was nothing more than a statistical calculating device, even if a sophisticated one.

In 1970 Professor Thomas S. Barthel, Director of the Ethnological Institute at the University of Tübingen, published the preliminary results of two years of research based on the studies of Victoria de la Jara.[19] He interpreted the ornamentation on pottery and robes as an ancient Peruvian system of words and signs, which he claimed to have partially deciphered. Barthel's theory was that this script was developed some 250 years before the Spanish conquest, but was forgotten during the period of colonial dominion. It consisted, he maintained, of about 400 different, multi-coloured and geometrically shaped signs, of which he believed he could read 24 with certainty and make a good guess at 50 more. In his view the Inca script was akin to early First Dynasty hieroglyphics in Egypt: ideograms strung together in a sort of telegraphese. Since Barthel reached these conclusions, however, no further advance has been made in interpreting the Inca 'script', and we can only hope that this very promising prelude will lead to something useful.

As in the pre-Inca period, it was natural for jewellery, ornaments and fine clothing to be reserved for the privileged class. Whereas the clothes of the lower classes were purely functional and almost unornamented, the Inca and his numerous wives wore magnificent dresses woven by the 'Virgins of the Sun' that could compete with the costumes of any European king or emperor. Particularly remarkable were their robes decorated with multi-coloured feathers from tropical birds, which amazed the Spaniards. A simple plain weave cotton fabric formed the base. On this the feathers of parrots, ducks, herons and other birds with colourful plumage were attached, by the bent quill, to two cotton threads running across the base material of the same yarn so close-packed that there was absolutely no space left between them.

Using this very old technique, which had already been employed in Nazca and Middle Horizon textiles, the artists produced not only robes (*Pl. 177*), but also headdresses

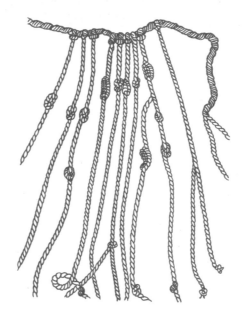

Figs. 97, 98 Part of a quipu, and Huaman Poma de Ayala's illustration of the Quipuca-mayoc.

and other accessories (*Pl. 183*). A surviving feather fabric with large square fields (*Pl. 178*) probably formed part of a wall-hanging used to decorate a temple or some other religious building. Some examples exist in which the smallest feathers measure only 6×11 mm. and are fitted together with no more than 1 mm. between them.[20] The degree of manual skill needed to produce such an object is almost unimaginable, and it is safe to infer that it could only be worn by someone of very high rank. What excites admiration is not only the technical expertise, at least equal to the finest filigree work in gold, but also the artistic merit of the colour composition. Figural motifs, too, are sometimes included. A magnificent poncho in the Lindenmuseum, Stuttgart, has two red felines flanking the usual step pattern on a light ground.[21]

In order to understand the great differences in the production, function and distribution of clothing, we must know something about the social order of this mighty, but comparatively shortlived, state. The ruling class was divided into three levels. The first comprised the 'imperial family', the kin of the reigning Inca. Only the members of this class were entitled to occupy the highest secular and religious offices. Next came the *curacas*, the nobility of conquered peoples, whom the Inca allowed to remain as officials and dignitaries for diplomatic reasons. A third category, sometimes with more power than the *curacas*, was the 'nobility of merit'. These nobles were of common birth, but belonged to the clan of the reigning Inca dynasty and had acquired their rank by rendering special services. Like the Inca, they wore earplugs as a sign of rank.

At the bottom of the social ladder were the *yanacuna*, who had no rights and no property. They were too low to be recorded by the keepers of the knotted strings, the officials of the empire, and even Spanish chroniclers made only a passing reference to them. Slightly higher were the *llacta runa*, a large body who formed the backbone of the state. The exact translation of this Quechua word is 'villagers'; it means primarily the farmers belonging to conquered tribes. The officials recorded them on the *quipus* and the Tucuiricuc or 'All-Seeing', a high official of the Inca, controlled the tribute they paid:

Fig. 99 A hunchbacked woman, spinning as she walks along. From the chronicle of Huaman Poma de Ayala.

agricultural products, weapons or tools and fabrics, of which church and state each demanded a third. The villager was only allowed to keep one third, preventing him and his family from leading anything but a very meagre existence. However, the state supplied this class with free clothing. On his wedding-day every citizen was entitled to two garments – one for everyday use and one for holidays.

The following description of the clothing worn by ancient Peruvian highlanders comes from a chronicler of the early colonial period, Lope de Atienza:[22]

Generally the Indians go barefoot, with bare arms and legs, and instead of a smock or shirt they wear an item of clothing they call *cuzma*, which we would describe as a kind of short shirt. It is cut just like a corn sack and has two slits at the sides for putting the arms through and a slit above for the head; it reaches down to the knees. As an over-garment they take thin cotton cloths about two and a half ells long and two ells wide . . . The women also differ greatly in their clothing. Mostly they make a miserable and not very clean impression and cover themselves only with two cloths. They wind one of them round their bodies, wrap pretty brightly coloured bands like straps round it and fasten it over the breast with two fairly large silver or copper clasps or pins. Thus they walk about, do their work, cover themselves at night and attire themselves by day. The more attractive women take pains to make themselves cleaner and tidier, because they know that it will bring them some return; but those poor creatures who are only there to serve their husband, work in his fields and rear his children walk about in such a dirty and dishevelled condition that it is miserable to behold. Their dress covers the top half of their legs and one could take them for roadmenders, except that they wear no stockings. They take great pleasure in pins and clasps and so they wear them on the breast to improve the appearance of their wretched clothing.

The robes used in religious ceremonies were quite different. We have a detailed description, attributed to the Jesuit Father Blas Valera:[23]

On the most important feast days he came to the temple of the great Illa Tecce, the Sun God or the God Pirua, to scatter incense or bring a sacrifice or some other gift. For this he dressed in the following way: on his head he wore a large tiara in the form of a hood which went over his ears, the *vila chucu*. On this he laid all kinds of jewellery, such as a gold mock ducat, worked in the form of the sun, and a large diadem. Below the chin he wore a half-moon-shaped ornamental gold piece and above on his head waved long feathers from the large parrots known as *guacamayas*. All this was trimmed with small gold platelets and precious stones. The whole tiara with all its ornaments was called *huampar chucu*. Then came a loose flowing cassock without sleeves or belt, a kind of tunic which reached to the ground, and over that a *huapil*, a kind of sleeveless

Figs. 100, 101   Two women of a poorer class spinning outside a hut, and a young woman working at the belt loom (cp. p. 233). From the chronicle of Huaman Poma de Ayala.

surplice of white wool, reaching to the knees, with red woollen fringes and borders. The whole *huapil* was trimmed with small gold platelets and precious stones. Instead of sleeves he wore bangles and bracelets of gold and precious stones, and his footwear was of fine wool . . .

The clothing of the 'All-Seeing', who travelled through the country with a numerous retinue as representative of the Inca, made a great impression on the common people. He wore the usual garment hanging over the shoulders (*yacolla*), which in his case was gleaming yellow ornamented with small gold platelets and brightly coloured feathers. Underneath he had a dark blue *unku* trimmed with red tassels on the right shoulder as a symbol of blood and the colour of life. Instead of red tassels he wore white when he went to the wedding of a high dignitary and black when he had to represent his sovereign at an important funeral. It was also this official's duty to decide which of the village girls aged between eight and nine would be suitable as an *aclla cuna*, one of the 'chosen virgins'. In his *Comentarios reales*, the chronicler Garcilaso de la Vega (son of a Spanish soldier and an Inca princess) has this to say about these Virgins of the Sun:

In spite of their paganism and their hollow idolatry, the Inca kings had some remarkable institutions. One of them was the vow of perpetual chastity taken by women in the many religious houses constructed for them in nearly every province in the empire. So that people may understand what this meant for the women, the occupations they devoted themselves to and how they spent their time, let it all be set down here . . .

Here we particularly want to speak of the house at Cuzco, because later it became the model for the other houses throughout Peru. A part of that city is called Acllahuasi, 'House of the Chosen' . . . Between it and the temple of the Sun lay another large housing complex and also the large square in front of the Temple. This clearly shows how wrong the historians were in saying that these virgins lived in the Temple of the Sun, were its priestesses and helped the priests during sacrifices. There was in fact such a great distance between the two houses . . . and it was one of the main principles of those Inca kings that no man was allowed entrance to the house of the nuns and no woman into the Temple of the Sun. That house was called the 'House of the Chosen' for the women were chosen for their origins and their beauty. They had to be virgins and so for safety's sake only children of eight and under were selected. . . . As a general rule there were more than five hundred of these nuns, but the number was not limited . . . there were others who looked after the novices and instructed them in the practices of their idolatry and in skills such as spinning, weaving and sewing . . .

193

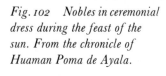

Fig. 102   Nobles in ceremonial dress during the feast of the sun. From the chronicle of Huaman Poma de Ayala.

The description throws a significant light on the position of the Virgins of the Sun, whose duties included the preparation of the yarn (*Fig. 104*) and the production of most of the Inca's sumptuous robes. Such items were in very great demand, for an Inca never wore a garment more than once. In addition there was the rich clothing made for the high officials, the nobility around the Inca, his sister-wife and his chosen concubines. In principle these garments were constructed like those of the lower classes – not tailored, but woven in individual widths and bands, borders, fringes, tassels, etc., which were then sewn together to make shirts, coats or mantles. The difference between the shirt of the common man (*Pl. 181*) and that of a person of high rank usually lay in the brilliant colours of the latter, the scrupulous execution, the composition of the motifs, the quality of the dye and the material for the yarn, only finely spun alpaca or vicuña wool being used. The natural fat content of the wool gave the cloth a matt silky sheen, which explains why the *conquistadores* spoke of the fine 'silky' clothing of the Inca nobles. The Inca emblem of dignity was a broad coloured band wrapped round the head several times, the *llantu*, from which hung a tassel with fringes, the *mascapaicha*, and two feathers of a very rare bird, the *corquenque*, which only the reigning monarch was allowed to wear. The headgear of the nobility was varied and indicated not only rank and position, but also the region in which the personage exercised his office. The chequerboard pattern in *Plate 182* was the badge of exceptional warriors or high-ranking commanders.

Other items worn by the Inca himself were gaiter bands, a kind of protection for knee and ankle; a shirtlike undergarment woven of the finest vicuña wool, reaching to the knees; a broad brocade belt round the waist, the *tocapu*, holding the undergarment together; and a cape-like shoulder covering ornamented with rich embroidery and applied bits of gold or shell (cf. *Pl. 175*, the ceremonial garment of a high dignitary, which is completely covered with small gold platelets attached to loops). With every step the wearer took, the sun flashed and sparkled on the hundreds of eighteen-carat gold discs, which also jingled impressively.

Figs. 103, 104 High-ranking
Indian women, shown wearing
cloaks fastened with pins; on the
left, the third wife of Capac
Umit, and on the right, a Virgin
of the Sun. From the chronicle of
Huaman Poma de Ayala.

The dress of the *coya*, the Inca's principal wife, was distinguished by strong colouring and the special quality of the material. Her undergarment, the *acsu*, was of no specified colour. The cloak (*jlíclla*), shorter than its male counterpart, was held together at breast height with a silver or gold pin (*tupu*), as with the women of other classes, except that their pins were made of cheaper materials (*Fig. 103*). Even today the Indian highland women hold their shoulder cloths together in a very similar way. The *coya*, too, wore a wide headband with a feather or a flower, usually of sheet gold, as a sign of her high rank.

On the question of what happened to all this sumptuous clothing the chroniclers do not agree. Some state that the servants collected everything, whether it was the remains of food on plates used only once by the Inca or an item of clothing worn by him only once, and ceremonially burnt them on one special day of the year. Garcilaso de la Vega maintains, on the contrary, that 'There were also plentiful supplies of new clothing both for daily use and for the bed; for the Inca never wore his clothes twice, but gave them to his relations. All his bedclothes were woven of vicuña wool, which is so fine that Philip II had it brought to Europe for his bed, together with other Peruvian products.'

The gulf between the different classes in the Inca empire was unbridgeable. The pomp and splendour which surrounded the head of the dynasty, his enormous harem, and the golden gardens in which everything from the cobs of maize to the butterflies was reproduced in gold and glittered whatever the season – all this could not disguise the fact that the greatest and most powerful ruler of ancient America was nothing but a lonely prisoner of the religious and political structure created by his ancestors. It was this very absolutism – the unapproachability of the god-king who exacted absolute obedience from all his subjects which none dared gainsay – that led to the astonishingly rapid collapse of the empire. 'In my empire no bird flies and no leaf rustles if I do not wish it', claimed the last Inca, Atahualpa. When on 15 November 1532 the Spanish conqueror Francisco Pizarro with barely 200 men confronted some 20,000 Indian

195

Fig. 105   A highly stylized human face, on a slit tapestry probably made on the Central Coast at the time of the Inca invasions. (Völkerkunde-museum, Munich)

166 *A slit tapestry fragment showing two hybrid creatures of uncertain meaning, combining features of bird and fish (see pp. 20 and 156). Chancay valley, c. 1300–1532.*

warriors and literally drove the Inca from his throne, the event was inconceivable to his subjects. The 'white gods' proved superior to their god-king, the brain and heart of the mighty Inca state. The confused Indians allowed themselves to be captured without resistance. This sealed the fate of the empire.

The Europeans enjoyed only the briefest glimpse of the mighty Inca Empire in full flower. Within a few years the great cities had decayed and the art of the ancient Indians lapsed into oblivion. Centuries passed before archaeologists were to rediscover them. Then on the Central and to an even greater extent on the South Coast they found in the vicinity of former rest-houses and barracks and along the imperial Inca roads many graves containing textiles with all their original colours and vivid patterns. Even so, by a strange paradox, much less has survived from the Inca period, the nearest to us in time, than from the very much older and more longlived cultures. The finds from the last hundred years of pre-Columbian history represent only a small part of those astonishing textile products which, taken together, can recreate for us three millennia of the ancient Indians' art and way of life.

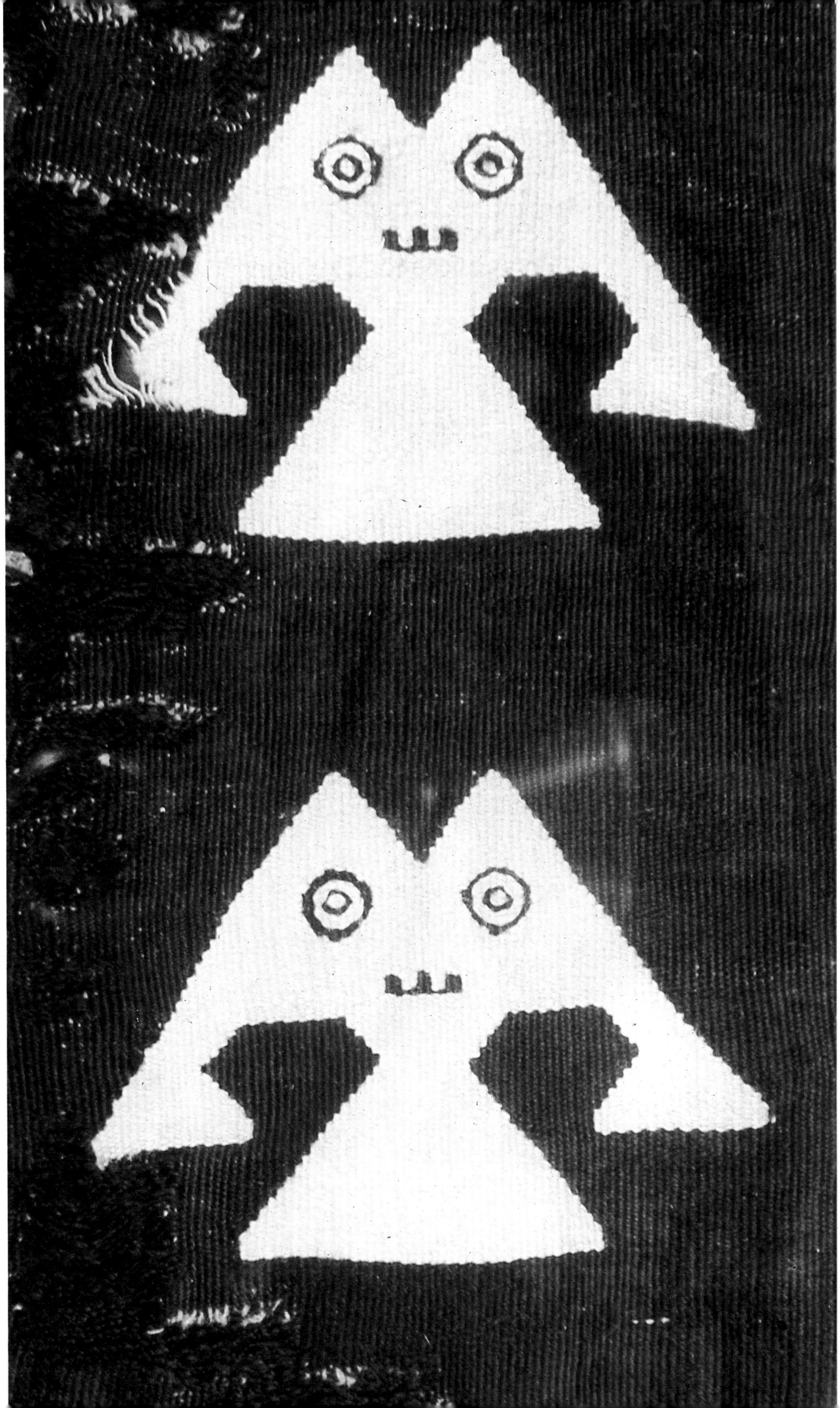

170

170 *The Inca 'morning star' motif alternating with a traditional bird pattern, in rep with supplementary brocading. South Coast, c. 1300–1532.*

171 *Textile with stripes in various techniques showing patterns common in the Inca period. In spite of the rigid geometricization, there are still echoes of a much older tradition. South or Central Coast, c. 1300–1532.*

172 *Textile fragments with different geometric motifs, including the 'leaf' representing featherwork. Central and South Coast, c. 1300–1532.*

171

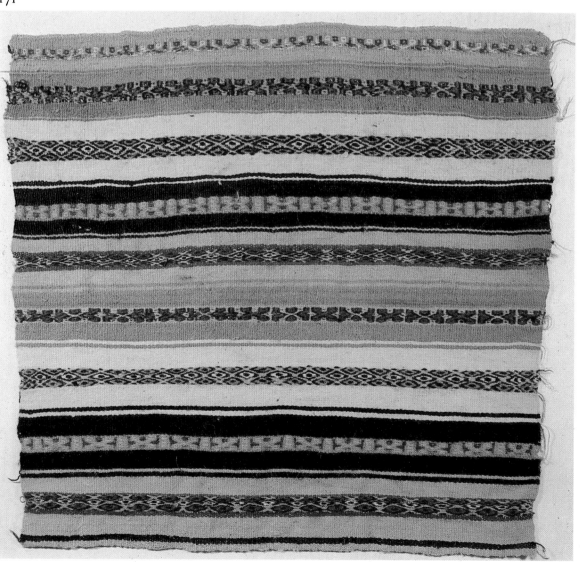

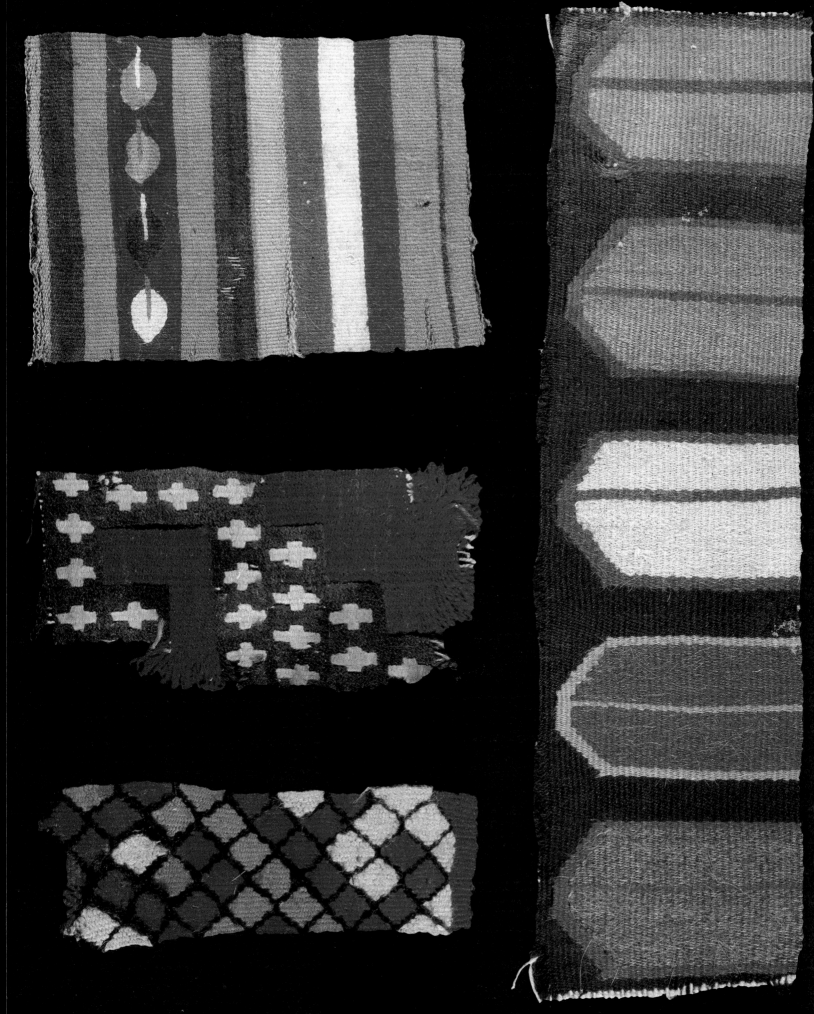

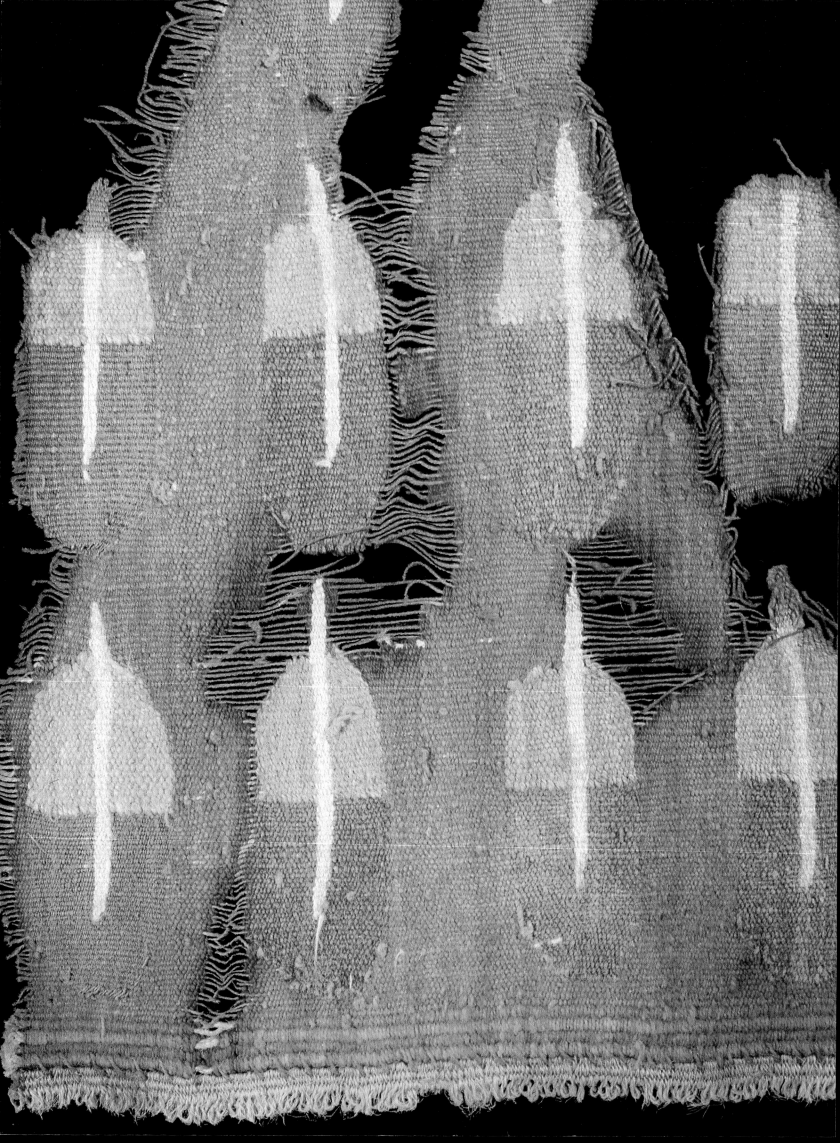

173 *Slit tapestry with the leaf motif imitating sewn-on feathers. Probably Central Coast, c. 1300–1532.*

174 *Tapestry poncho with bold geometric decoration. South Coast, Ica valley, c. 1400–1532.*

175 Large silk tapestry with
an abstract field crossed by
narrow stripes containing birds:
these small birds, which also
appear in the borders, constantly
recur in the Inca period, a
survival from earlier times.
Chancay, c. 1400–1532.

176 *Ceremonial robe of a high dignitary, covered with 18-carat gold platelets, sewn to loops on the polychrome textile ground. A central band with a lozenge pattern enclosing tightly sewn-on gold masks marks a still point in the restlessly shimmering, tinkling surface. Chimu-Inca, c. 1400–1532.*

176

177 *Feather poncho of a high dignitary. Both front and back are closely covered with feathers, held in place in the weave by their bent-back quills. South Coast, Pre-Inca or Early Inca, c. 1300–1532.*

178 *Part of a large feather fabric which may have served as a wall-hanging; this detail is about 79 cm. wide. South Coast (?), c. 1400–1532.*

Overleaf:

179 *Short shirt, in slit tapestry. Central Coast, Huacho, Pre-Inca or Early Inca, c. 1000–1532.*

178 *Part of a large feather fabric which may have served as a wall-hanging; this detail is about 79 cm. wide. South Coast (?), c. 1400–1532.*

179 *Short shirt, in slit tapestry. Central Coast, Huacho, Pre-Inca or Early Inca, c. 1000–1532.*

183 *Headdress and ruff of featherwork and silver sheet, which formed part of the ceremonial costume of a high dignitary of the Inca period. South Coast, c. 1470–1532.*

183

Fig. 106   A startled cat, on a
slit tapestry from the Central
Coast, c. 700–1000. Tiahuanaco influence is present, but the
motif lacks the severity of classic
Middle Horizon textiles.

Notes to the Text

Details of publications will be found in the Select Bibliography, pp. 231–3.

1 This information is chiefly based on the work of the Canadian archaeologist Richard S. MacNeish, published in 'Early Man in the Andes' (1971, in *Readings from Scientific American: Early Man in America*) and *The Central Peruvian Prehistoric Interaction Sphere*.

2 William H. Holmes, 'Textile Fabrics of Ancient Peru', 1889.

3 I am endebted to Henning Bischof, director of the excavations, for this information.

4 Only one of the many ancient American languages has a word for 'art'.

5 Junius B. Bird, who died in April 1982, was no mere 'footnote' to archaeology. He was a distinguished archaeologist, who did much to illuminate the obscure early period of Peruvian prehistory. He was a wonderful man, with a fine sense of humour, always unselfishly ready to give advice or help to young archaeologists, among them myself. He generously allowed me to use many illustrations taken from his models in this book. My heartfelt thanks, Don Junius!

6 There are two kinds of cotton, a lesser one with 13 chromosomes and a shrublike plant with 32 chromosomes. Both were confined to a few small cultivable areas. It is not known whether they were developed independently in Peru or whether one or both was introduced by settlers who came to the Peruvian coast from southern Ecuador.

7 See Bennett and Bird, 1964, and Conklin, 1971.

8 During excavations at Chavín de Huántar in 1965–6 Peruvian archaeologists found remarkable ceramics with many stylistic differences in the 'Rocas' and the 'Ofrendas gallery'. Lumbreras and Amat accordingly named the ceramic styles 'Chavín Ofrendas', which corresponds roughly to the Cupisnique style on the coast, and 'Chavín Rocas', which is divided into three phases and corresponds roughly to the classic flowering of the Chavín culture (*c.* 1000–500 BC). The stylistic features of ceramics, combined with their chronological sequence, often provide the most valuable clues for a study of textiles. There are very few surviving textiles from Chavín, and virtually none from the Highlands.

9 The search for the antecedents of the Chavín culture has so far proved inconclusive. Japanese archaeologists have played a significant role in extending knowledge of the Initial Period (notably through the excavation of Kotosh), but have not been able to discover where and when the distinguishing features emerged. D. W. Lathrap's finds in the Upper Amazon basin (known as Early Tutishcainyo) support his guess that the origins of the ceramic development are to be found in a still unknown phase and a still unexplored region in the rain forest east of the Andes (see Benson, ed., *Dumbarton Oaks Conference on Chavín*). Even if they do not give definitive answers, the Dumbarton Oaks Conference papers and Chiaki Kano's *Origins of the Chavín Culture*, 1979, are richly rewarding.

10 A reference to this interpretation may be contained in an old prayer from a later period addressed to Viracocha, the god of creation, which survived in the oral tradition long enough to be recorded by a Spanish chronicler. See Anton, *Altindianische Weisheit und Poesie*, p. 91.

11 'Carhua' has been variously spelt. Sawyer calls it 'Corowa' and also 'Carawa'. Lapiner, who came into possession of some of these precious textiles, calls it 'Carowa'. Tello, the first person to publish information about the site, called it 'Karwa'. Carhua has been ceaselessly plundered. Nothing is known of the context in which the textiles were found (whether with other artefacts, etc.), and it is not even known whether the site was a burial ground or a small settlement.

12 Nazca culture has traditionally been divided, on the basis of stylistic characteristics in ceramics, into nine phases or periods. I prefer the simpler division proposed by Sawyer, into Early, Middle, and Late Nazca (see the Chronological Table, p. 229). Early Nazca is preceded by the Proto-Nazca phase, the traditional period between the Paracas and Nazca cultures, by the end of which all the essential features existed. I also follow Sawyer in excluding Nazca 9, or Nazca-Huari: the superimposition of the alien Huari style is by then so strong that this phase must be classified as Middle Horizon.

13 Quechua, or 'Runa Simi' ('the language of men'), as many Peruvian Indians call it, is used colloquially today by several million people, mainly the highland Indians, in Peru, Ecuador, and parts of Bolivia.

14 Cabello de Balboa, in *Miscellanea Antarctica*, Lima 1920.

15 See G. Kutscher, *Chimu: Eine altindianische Hochkultur*, Berlin 1950, p. 96.

16 e.g. Antonio de la Calancha, *Corónica moralizada del orden de San Augustín en el Perú* (Barcelona 1638); Miguel Cabello de Balboa (1576–86; see note 14, above); and also Bartolomé de las Casas's compilation, *De las antiguas gentes del Perú*.

17 'Sapa Inca' or 'Sapay Inca' was the name of the supreme ruler, the 'Only Inca', 'Son of the Sun' and 'Benefactor of the Poor'. It has become customary to call all the inhabitants of the empire (especially those who spoke the imperial language, Quechua) Incas, but originally the name applied only to the original small group who, starting from the Cuzco valley, rapidly established the only Indian empire in ancient America.

18 Pedro Cieza de León, *La Crónica del Peru*. The work is in three volumes. The first contains the observations of the author, who served in Peru as a simple soldier; completed in 1550, it was published in Seville in 1553. (An English translation was published by the Hakluyt Society, London (no. 33, 1864): *The Travels of Pedro de Cieza de León, A. D. 1532–1550, Contained in the First Part of His Chronicle of Peru*.) The second volume deals with the history of the Incas and with the population shortly before the Spanish conquest, while the third covers the early colonial period; these were published in Madrid in 1880 and 1887. Among several subsequent editions is one in the Biblioteca de Autores Españoles, Madrid 1947.

19 *Verhandlungen des XXXVIII. Internationalen Amerikanisten-Kongress*, Munich 1970, vol. 2, pp. 237–42.

20 E. Yacovleff, 'Arte plumaria entre los antiquos Peruanos', in *Revista del Museo Nacional de Lima*, 1933, no. 2, p. 146.

21 Anton, *Alt-Amerika*, pl. 238.

22 *Compendio historial del estado de los Indios del Peru*, chapter 5. See also Baudin, 1961.

23 'Relación de los costumbres antiguas de los naturales del Pirú', in *Revista del Archivo Historico de Cuzco*, Lima 1953, no. 4.

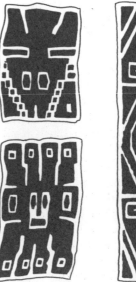

Figs. 107–109 Highly stylized hybrid creatures, on cotton textiles. Middle Horizon influence, c. 900–1200.

Notes on the Plates

When only a regional provenance is given, the exact site where an object was found is unknown. In measurements, height (as illustrated) precedes width.

1 Machu Picchu, east of Cuzco in the Urubumba valley, 2,200 m. above sea-level.
Southern Highlands, Inca culture, Late Horizon 1476–1532.

2 The restored ruins of Chuquitanta (El Paraíso), in the arid Chillón valley.
Central Coast, c. 2500–1800 BC.

3 Ruins of Chanchan.
North Coast, Chimu culture, Late Intermediate Period, c. 1000–1450.

4 Mummy bundle with false head.
Pachacamac, Central Coast, Late Intermediate Period, c. 1000–1470.
(Photo J. Alden Mason)

5 Polychrome vessel in the shape of a man's head.
Southern Highlands, Tiahuanaco culture, Middle Horizon, c. 500–700.
Height 15 cm.
Museo Nacional de Arqueología, La Paz, Bolivia

6 Double spout and bridge vessel with painted hand motif.
South Coast, Nazca culture, Early Intermediate Period, c. 100–600.
Height 13 cm.
Milwaukee Public Museum, Wisconsin

7 Mochica vessel in the shape of a seated man holding an *unku*.
North Coast, Moche culture, Early Intermediate Period, c. 100–600.
Height 18 cm.
Lindenmuseum, Stuttgart

8 Stirrup-spout vessel in the shape of a crouching man. His headgear with ear flaps and his striking features are characteristic of highland Indians.
North Coast, Moche culture, Early Intermediate Period, c. 100–600.
Height 19 cm.
Formerly B. P. Collection

9 Painted plain weave cotton fabric, probably part of a wall-hanging for a religious assembly room, with dots and two hand motifs placed one above the other.
South Coast, Chavinoid Paracas phase of the Paracas culture, Early Horizon, c. 1200–700 BC.
Detail c. 40×25 cm.
Staatliche Museen, Museum für Völkerkunde, West Berlin

10 Loom with unfinished pattern band.
Central Coast, Chancay, Late Intermediate Period, c. 1000–1450.
Height c. 60 cm.
Deutsches Museum, Munich

11 Mummy mask. Painted plain weave cotton cloth. This textile, only apparently incomplete, with its extended untrimmed warp threads which are rolled into balls, loops or cords, forms a kind of 'protective spirit' or 'guardian of the mummy bundle'. Such masks were originally sewn on to the outer mummy wrapping with large stitches (cf. Fig. 32 and Pls. 40–42). This function determined form and content, but allowed freedom of execution. The motif, here a mythical creature surrounded by a double-headed jagged snake, is in an attitude reminiscent of the Chavín Staff God. The warp threads, still wrapped round the warp beam, are divided in the middle and wound round a pad of raw cotton, forming a kind of 'head ornament' for the guardian figure, an impression enhanced by the sewn-on feathers.
South Coast, Paracas culture (Ocucaje Phase 9–10), Early Horizon, c. 500 BC.
42×30 cm.
Private collection

12 Border of a burial cloth showing a warrior, his garment decorated with trophy heads, holding the severed head of an enemy. Covering stem stitch embroidery in alpaca wool on plain weave cotton fabric.
South Coast, Paracas culture, Early Horizon, c. 400–200 BC.
Height c. 12 cm.
Textile Museum, Washington, D.C.

13 Highly stylized demons' heads decorating a burial mantle diagonally. The ground cloth is largely destroyed. Cross-knit

loop stitch embroidery in wool worked around cotton base.
South Coast, Nazca culture, Early Intermediate Period,
c. 100 BC–AD 500.
Detail c. 30×24 cm.
Edward H. Merrin Gallery, New York

14 Textile fragment showing four men, seafaring warriors or
fishermen, confronting each other in martial attitudes in two
boats. The numerous animals surrounding them, some in their
natural forms, others as hybrids, reflect both the real and the imaginary worlds of the weavers. Slit tapestry, wool on cotton warp.
North Coast, Moche or Chimu culture, Early or Late Intermediate Period, c. 300–700 or c. 1000–1450.
30.5×26 cm.
Edward H. Merrin Gallery, New York

15 Richly decorated slit tapestry. In addition to the colour, its
effect is enhanced by varying weave-structures (areas of openwork), inset (stitched in) arches, and projecting tassels and
fringes. A three-dimensional effect is achieved by the decorative
trimmings. Wool on cotton with trimmings and other decorative
elements of wool.
South Coast, Tiahuanaco-Huari style, c. 700–1000.
Complete fabric c. 35×38 cm.
Private collection, London

16 Detail of a slit tapestry border with birds of prey.
South Coast, Tiahuanaco-Huari style, c. 700–1000.
Size of motif c. 4.5×7 cm.
Private collection, London

17 Ornamental band with waterfowl, facing in opposite directions. Wool brocade on rep of wool on cotton warp.
North Coast, Chimu style (?), Late Intermediate Period,
c. 1000–1460.
c. 6×13 cm.
Private collection

18 Stylized sea bird in a rectangular field worked in wool brocade on plain weave cotton fabric.
Central or North Coast, Late Intermediate Period, c. 1000–1460.
c. 12×16 cm.
Private collection

19 Small coca bag with striped pattern and abstract bird motif.
Tapestry with brocaded side borders and plaited multicoloured
cord.
South Coast, Tiahuanaco-Huari style, c. 700–1000.
8×7 cm., length of cord 38 cm.
Private collection, London

20, 21 Front and back of a brocaded plain weave fabric; cotton
and alpaca wool.
    Brocaded textiles are very similar seen from the front, and it is
often hard to distinguish between them. On the back it is clear
that the coloured pattern threads were drawn through to form
the pattern during weaving, and as they turn back and forth they
show an outline of the pattern. The ground is generally provided
by a plain cotton fabric.
North Coast (?), Chimu culture (?), c. 1000–1450.
c. 10×13 cm.
Lindenmuseum, Stuttgart

22 Openwork gauze with a pattern of cats and birds.
    Openwork fabrics of this kind are mostly made of strongly
overtwisted cotton yarn and are constructed with the help of a
frame which can be removed later, allowing 'scaffolding
threads' to be stretched over the whole square or rectangular
surface. The net weaving, especially the complicated figure in-
sertion, required several processes. Undyed cotton.
Central Coast, Chancay style, Late Intermediate Period,
c. 1000–1400.
c. 37×30.5 cm.
Private collection

23 Feather fabric showing a face. For the technique, see the note
to Pl. 177.
South Coast, Late Intermediate Period, c. 1000–1450 (possibly
earlier).
Featherwork 18×22 cm.
Milwaukee Public Museum, Wisconsin

24 Painted cotton fabric, probably part of a wall-hanging.
Central Coast, Chancay (?), Late Intermediate Period,
c. 1000–1400.
55×194 cm.
Stolper Galleries, London (formerly Munich)

25 Large textile, probably part of a wall-hanging, with a field of
chequerwork interrupted near the top by a horizontal border.
The bottom of the fabric terminates in a second decorative
border. The fabric is decorated with bird motifs in different techniques (plain weave, slit tapestry, etc.); cotton and wool.
Central Coast, Chancay style, Late Intermediate Period,
c. 1000–1200.
Complete fabric 116×152 cm.
André Emmerich Gallery Inc., New York

26 Man's sleeveless shirt (unku) with ornamental border fringes.
In addition to the harmonious integration of colours, the Peruvian weavers knew how to combine different weaves with great
skill and so enhance the aesthetic attraction of even a simple garment. Plain weave ground, cotton and wool, wool borders and
fringes, slit tapestry and brocading threads.
Probably South Coast, Late Intermediate Period or Late
Horizon, c. 1000–1500.
c. 50×55 cm.
Private collection, London

27 Side of the main pyramid at Chavín de Huántar.
Northern Highlands, Chavín culture, c. 1200–400 BC.

28 Painted cotton fabric, probably part of a wall-hanging.
Callango (?), Chavinoid Paracas phase of the Paracas culture,
c. 1200–700 BC.
c. 35×40 cm.
Museo Nacional de Antropología y Arqueología, Lima

29 Relief slab from the temple complex at Chavín de Huántar.
Northern Highlands, Chavín culture, c. 1200–400 BC.
Height c. 50 cm.
Private collection

30 Detail of a painted cotton fabric.
South Coast, Carhua (Karwa), Chavinoid Paracas phase of the

Paracas culture, *c.* 1200–700 BC.
Height of figure *c.* 15 cm.
Museo Amano, Lima

31 Figurative border details from a burial cloth. Three-dimensional cross-knit loop stitch embroidery of coloured wool worked around a preformed cotton base.

Textile design is the most conservative of all the Peruvian 'arts', and an attempt to establish a clear typology of the various Paracas phases up to Proto-Nazca is not helped by the fact that almost all textiles have come from grave robberies and are thus without an archaeological context. It therefore seemed preferable to group this and the following plates thematically rather than according to an unestablished chronology.
South Coast, Late Paracas/Proto-Nazca, *c.* 300–100 BC.
Height of figures *c.* 4–5 cm.
Private collection

32 Petroglyph in the Alto de la Guitarra pass. The deity holds a small fish in its claws as a trophy.
North Coast, Chavín style, *c.* 1200–700 BC.

33 The feline motif, here with the attributes of the bird of prey (beak) and snake symbols, as pattern on a painted plain weave cotton fabric.
South Coast, Carhua (Karwa), Chavinoid Paracas phase of the Paracas culture, *c.* 1200–700 BC.
Detail *c.* 30×24 cm.
Private collection, Lima

34 Stylized feline heads in coloured wool embroidery on an undyed cotton fabric.
South Coast, probably Early Paracas, early Callango style, *c.* 700–500 BC.
Size of one figure *c.* 5×4.5 cm.
Odeon Galerie, Munich

35 Inside of bowl incised with a highly stylized feline motif.
South Coast, Early Paracas, Callango style, *c.* 700–500 BC.
Diameter 22 cm.
The Nathan Cummings Collection, Textile Museum, Washington, D.C.

36 'Reconstruction' of a painted cotton fabric in the classic Chavín style. Señora Alva y Alva of the Museo Bruning in Lambayeque transferred the motif of the feline god from a stone relief in the Northern Highlands to cloth. The copy brings out the many faces of the god of the Early Horizon.
50×75 cm.

37 Cotton fabric with painting showing waterfowl (see also endpapers).
South Coast, Late Paracas/Proto-Nazca, *c.* 300–100 BC.
43×98 cm.
André Emmerich Gallery Inc., New York

38 A small fragment of a border with fringes, depicting trophy heads. Cross-knit loop stitch embroidery in wool on a cotton base; fringes of twisted thread loops.
South Coast, Late Paracas/Proto-Nazca, *c.* 300–100 BC.
14×19.5 cm.
André Emmerich Gallery Inc., New York

39 Detail of a decorative band on a burial mantle or robe; the ceremonial staves or weapons, as well as the sumptuous garment of this figure reminiscent of the Chavín Staff God, are ornamented with the severed heads of enemies. Wool and cotton slit tapestry. The designs were originally outlined in black, but this dye, which obviously contained acids, destroyed the weft threads (an unusual occurrence in Peru), giving the false impression that this textile was worked discontinuously.
South Coast, Late (?) Nazca culture, *c.* 400–600.
Detail *c.* 30×24 cm.
Private collection, London

40 The beginnings of an independent tradition are found on the painted cotton textiles known as mummy masks. Here the stylized face of a man is depicted with two felines as face painting. Plain weave fabric; salmon pink background with dark blue painting.
South Coast, Paracas (Ocucaje phase 9–10), *c.* 500 BC.
Complete fabric 81.5×28.3 cm.
Textile Museum, Washington, D.C.

41, 42 Two 'mummy masks' painted with semi-human and semi-animal monsters vaguely reminiscent in their attitude of the Chavín Staff God.
South Coast, Paracas (Ocucaje phase 9–10), *c.* 500 BC.
30×30 cm.; 30×24 cm.
Textile Museum, Washington, D.C.

43 Detail of a fragment of an ornamental border of a burial cloth with mythical figures showing both zoomorphic (felines and snakes) and anthropomorphic attributes. Covering stem stitch embroidery in alpaca wool on a cotton fabric.

In the Middle Paracas period new techniques began to emerge on the South Coast which facilitated a rich artistic development in textile art, among them covering stem stitch embroidery: at first only the edge of cotton fabrics was ornamented. The motifs on these embroidered borders closely resemble the painted mythical figures.
South Coast, Middle Paracas, *c.* 500–300 BC.
Complete fragment 23×13 cm.
Private collection

44 Detail of a burial cloth border ornamented with a row of figures in cult costume. Covering stem stitch embroidery in wool on plain weave cotton fabric.
South Coast, Late Paracas/Proto-Nazca, *c.* 300–100 BC.
Height of figure *c.* 12 cm.
Museo Nacional de Antropología y Arqueología, Lima

45 Fragment of a border decorated with demonic masks, still under the influence of the prevailing Chavín cult. Covering stem stitch embroidery in wool on plain weave cotton fabric.
South Coast, Middle Paracas, *c.* 500–300 BC.
Height of detail *c.* 30 cm.
Textile Museum, Washington, D.C.

46 Corner of a burial cloth with the feline motif. Covering stem stitch embroidery in wool on plain weave cotton fabric.
South Coast, Middle–Late Paracas, *c.* 500–200 BC.
Detail *c.* 16×16 cm.
Textile Museum, Washington, D.C.

47 Part of a border showing a hybrid demon with catlike features, a constantly recurring theme of Paracas-Nazca mythology. Covering stem stitch embroidery in wool on plain weave cotton fabric.
South Coast, Late Paracas, *c.* 300–200 BC.
Detail *c.* 7.5×8 cm
Private collection

48, 49 Five borders from robes or burial mantles. Four are embroidered with different representations of birds, some of them very realistic; one shows anthropomorphic monkey demons holding a snake in their claws. The same technique of covering stem stitch embroidery is used in all.
South Coast, Late Paracas/Proto-Nazca, *c.* 300–100 BC.
Total length of individual borders between *c.* 60 and 110 cm., width between *c.* 8 and 12 cm.
Textile Museum, Washington, D.C.

50 Detail of a border depicting two intertwined snakes; the empty areas are filled with lizards and mice. Cotton fabric, fringes and embroidery in covering stem stitch using alpaca wool (pink, beige, light and dark brown, moss green, blue and dark blue).
South Coast, Late Paracas, *c.* 300–200 BC.
Detail *c.* 18×65 cm.
Textile Museum, Washington, D.C.

51 Ornamental border depicting a group of connected figures forming a mythical creature, a later variation of the demon seen on painted 'mummy masks' in the Ocucaje style (Pls. 41, 42). While the imagery of this fragment is archaic, technically it appears to have been far ahead of its time: according to Junius B. Bird, we have here the only known Paracas style fabric produced by the tapestry technique.
    In this technique, which was to become the dominant mode, weavers could achieve nearly every pattern and colour they desired. Unlike slit tapestries, such textiles have no slits where wefts of different colours meet. That is usually achieved, as here, by alternate looping of the weft or interlocking around a common warp thread (see p. 230 (4)).
Alpaca weft on cotton warp.
South Coast, Late Paracas/Proto-Nazca, *c.* 300–100 BC.
Height *c.* 5 cm.
Textile Museum, Washington, D.C.

52 Two borders ornamented with birds, one with sea birds in a naturalistic style, the other with vulture-like birds and highly stylized mythical creatures (felines and apes) as fillers. Covering stem stitch embroidery in wool on plain weave cotton fabric.
South Coast, Middle–Late Paracas, *c.* 500–200 BC.
Width *c.* 6 cm.
Private collection

53 Ornamental band with highly stylized fish, embroidered in covering stem stitch.
South Coast, Middle–Late Paracas, *c.* 500–200 BC.
Width *c.* 3.5 cm.
Private collection

54 Fragment of plain weave cotton cloth with stem stitch embroidery in alpaca wool.
South Coast, Middle–Late Paracas, *c.* 500–200 BC.

c. 10×22 cm.
Textile Museum, Washington, D.C.

55 Cotton fabric with mythical figures painted in dark brown, probably a design sampler.
South Coast, Late Paracas/Proto-Nazca, *c.* 300–100 BC.
c. 38×92 cm.
Edward H. Merrin Gallery, New York

56 Two faces with ritual skin painting, from a border. Embroidered in cross-knit loop stitch, using wool dyed red, white, blue and black, on a preshaped cotton base; back and front match.
South Coast, Late Paracas/Proto-Nazca, *c.* 300–100 BC.
3.6×4.2 cm.; 3.9×4.2 cm.
Private collection

57 Part of the trimming of one of the undecorated, mostly rectangular indigo burial cloths. Three-dimensional cross-knit loop stitch embroidery in wool on cotton.
South Coast, Proto-Nazca–Early Nazca, *c.* 200 BC–AD 200.
Height of figure *c.* 11 cm., length of fragment *c.* 31 cm.
Private collection

58 The 'diver' motif, from a burial cloth. These 'falling figures' exhibit more human than animal features. That they were human sacrifices – women, according to their clothing – who were thrown into the water to propitiate the demons and gods cannot be proved, though the ribs of this figure suggest a sacrificial victim rather than a 'dancer' (see Pl. 59). Covering stem stitch embroidery on plain weave fabric, both of alpaca wool.
South Coast, Late Paracas/Proto-Nazca, *c.* 300–100 BC.
Height of figure *c.* 12 cm.; total size of cloth 213.5×44 cm.
Textile Museum, Washington, D.C.

59 Part of a border with 'dancing' warriors or warlike deities. Even after two thousand years the hand of a true artist is detectable: rapid movement is conveyed not only by the attitude of the body and the streaming hair, but also by the contrasted small figures. Everything is so delicately balanced that the flat surface seems to have acquired an extra dimension. Covering stem stitch embroidery in alpaca wool on plain weave fabric.
South Coast, Late Paracas/Proto-Nazca, *c.* 300–100 BC.
Length of figure *c.* 12 cm.
Museo Nacional de Antropología y Arqueología, Lima

60 Detail of the border of a burial mantle with the motif of a deity demanding sacrifices, as the trophy head in his claws indicates. Covering stem stitch embroidery in alpaca wool on plain weave cotton fabric.
South Coast, Late Paracas/Proto-Nazca, *c.* 300–100 BC.
Figure *c.* 13×15.5 cm.
Textile Museum, Washington, D.C.

61 Detail of a border showing zoomorphic creatures with feline characteristics. Covering stem stitch embroidery on cotton fabric.
South Coast, Late Paracas/Proto-Nazca, *c.* 300–100 BC.
Height of one figure *c.* 13 cm.
CDO Collection

62 Warriors holding weapons and trophy heads; the lower hem of their garments is ornamented with trophy heads. Embroidery in wool on cotton.

South Coast, Late Paracas/Proto-Nazca, c. 300–100 BC.
18×18 cm.
Private collection

63 Detail of an unfinished border depicting a vegetation god. In one hand it holds a *tumi*, and under its other arm a trophy head; a jagged snake's body terminating in a mythical creature emerges from its mouth. Covering stem stitch embroidery in wool on cotton fabric.
South Coast, Late Paracas/Proto-Nazca, c. 300–100 BC.
Width of border c. 10 cm.
Textile Museum, Washington, D.C.

64 Detail of a border showing a figure in the costume of a 'bird man'. Embroidery in wool on plain weave cotton fabric.
South Coast, Late Paracas/Proto-Nazca, c. 300–100 BC.
Height of figure c. 12 cm.
Private collection

65 Detail of a border with fringes. In textiles showing the 'man of action' warriors, priests and chieftains are depicted, always in imposing attitudes, which produce a very different effect from the sense of floating above reality that emanates from the mythical figures. The palette is still of striking beauty. Stem stitch embroidery in wool on cotton fabric.
South Coast, Late Paracas/Proto-Nazca, c. 300–100 BC.
Height of detail c. 10 cm.; width of border 7.7 cm.
Edward H. Merrin Gallery, New York

66 Pattern band with animals and hybrids, some of which are incomplete, found in a burial together with other grave goods. Embroidery in wool on a plain weave cotton band.
South Coast, Late Paracas/Proto-Nazca, c. 300–100 BC.
Length 126 cm., height of motifs 3–6 cm.
Private collection

67 Part of a border with mythical birds. Covering stem stitch embroidery in wool on plain weave cotton fabric.
South Coast, Middle–Late Paracas, c. 500–200 BC.
Height of figures c. 6 cm.
Edward H. Merrin Gallery, New York

68 Detail of the border of a burial cloth depicting a vegetation god. Covering stem stitch embroidery in wool.
South Coast, Late Paracas/Proto-Nazca, c. 300–100 BC.
Height c. 12 cm.
Museo Nacional de Antropología y Arqueología, Lima

69 Detail of a burial cloth with alternately plain and ornamented rectangular fields. Stem stitch embroidery in wool on plain weave cotton fabric.
South Coast, Late Paracas/Proto-Nazca, c. 300–100 BC.
Detail c. 35×35 cm.
Lindenmuseum, Stuttgart

70 A highly stylized Nazca deity with headdress and protruding tongue, repeated in alternating colours in ornamental bands of woollen slit tapestry on thin brown cotton fabric.
South Coast, Nazca, c. AD 100–600.
Height of figure c. 12 cm.
Private collection

71 Detail of a border in woollen slit tapestry. The carefully contrived 'divine image' (cp. Pl. 70), now represented only by the head, is repeated in the headdress, and the same mythical creature appears upside-down in different colouring.
South Coast, Nazca, c. AD 100–600.
Height c. 12 cm.
Private collection

72 Double spout and bridge vessel painted with an anthropomorphic feline deity.
South Coast, Nazca, c. AD 100–600.
Height 25.8 cm.
Private collection, Buenos Aires

73 Nose ornament of 18-carat sheet gold. Similar artefacts made of other materials help us to interpret the complicated images and symbols of textiles like those in Pl. 44.
South Coast, Nazca, c. AD 100–600.
23.8×21 cm.
Museo de Oro, Miguel Mujica Gallo Foundation, Lima

74 Two trophy heads.
South Coast, Nazca-Huari, c. 600–700.
Height 28 cm.; 22 cm.
Private collection, USA

75, 77 Large cloth, probably part of a wall-hanging. The plain weave ground consists of finely spun alpaca wool, dyed wine-red. Woven into it are cross-shaped patterns in thick alpaca-wool tapestry in alternating colours (yellow, orange, blue, white and black).
South Coast, Nazca-Huari, c. 600–700.
Complete fabric 310×150 cm., size of one motif c. 15×15 cm.
Textile Museum, Washington, D.C.

76 Fragment of an *unku* with geometric patterns and lobsters. Tapestry technique, using undyed and violet wool.
South Coast, Late Nazca, Huari influence, c. 600–700.
c. 60×25 cm.
Textile Museum, Washington, D.C.

78 Fragment, probably part of a man's sleeveless shirt, with a form of decoration most unusual in Peru: separate patches of cloth tie-dyed by the *plangi* method are sewn together at random.
South Coast, Late Nazca/Nazca-Huari, c. 600–700.
108×68 cm.
Private collection

79 Tapestry fragment with highly stylized figures broken up into rectangular forms, which are difficult to make out today but were no doubt readily comprehensible to the initiate.

It is not clear from archaeological finds whether Middle Horizon fabrics and garments, which were all found in graves on the coast, were imported from the highlands or made on the coast by weavers from the mountains. There are many indications that the garments were reserved for a specific class and expressed their rank in the social hierarchy. The traces of wear on many finds show that these textiles were not exclusively intended for the cult of the dead.
South Coast, Middle Horizon, c. 600–800.
46×39.5 cm.
Private collection, Switzerland

80 Façade of the Gateway of the Sun at Tiahuanaco.
Southern Highlands, classic Tiahuanaco style, c. 200–600.
Height 3 m., width 3.82 m., depth c. 45 cm.; height of frieze 82 cm.

81 Vessel with polychrome painting including a face with tear-marks.
South Coast style, c. 500–800.
Height 12 cm.
Private collection, Zurich

82 Polychrome painted beaker.
Southern Highlands, ruins of Tiahuanaco, classic Tiahuanaco style, c. 500–800.
Height 14 cm.
Museo Nacional de Arqueología, La Paz

83 Animal-headed vessel.
Southern Highlands, ruins of Tiahuanaco, classic Tiahuanaco style, c. 500–800.
Height 15 cm.
Formerly Fritz Buck Collection, La Paz

84 Stirrup spout vessel in the shape of an animal.
Central Coast style, c. 500–1000.
Height 16 cm.
Private collection, Zurich

85 Vessel with polychrome painting of a bird of prey.
Southern Highlands, ruins of Tiahuanaco, classic Tiahuanaco style, c. 500–800.
Height 9 cm.
Museo Nacional de Arqueología, La Paz

86 Miniature tunic in alpaca wool tapestry.
South Coast, Middle Horizon, c. 600–800.
22.5×31 cm.
Brooklyn Museum, New York, on loan from Mr and Mrs A. Bradley Martin

87 Tapestry fragment depicting the feline in cult clothing with ceremonial staff, sumptuous headdress and outspread wing-like cloak.
South Coast, Tiahuanaco-Huari style, c. 600–800.
c. 15×20 cm.
Textile Museum, Washington, D.C.

88 Detail of a man's garment in tapestry technique, alpaca on cotton warp.
South Coast, Tiahuanaco-Huari style, c. 600–800.
Size of one face of garment 106×105 cm.
Formerly CDO Collection

89 Tapestry fragment with the motif of the bird-headed staff-bearer.
South Coast, Tiahuanaco-Huari style, c. 600–800.
Size of figure 6.5×15.8 cm.
Private collection

90, 91 Painted bowl and detail of tapestry with the 'diagonal double motif'.

Since finds with a secure archaeological context are insufficient to establish an accurate textile chronology, it is impossible to say whether the diagonal double motif derives from the staff-bearer motif, as a reaction by weavers to the overloaded style of ornament which did not differentiate between the essential and the non-essential, or is an entirely independent development. At all events it changed textile imagery completely. Rejection of natural models gave the weavers unlimited scope to use their imagination. Never before or since have textile artists used abstraction so exhaustively or invented pure forms to represent actuality as they did with variations of this motif. A pair of reduced symbolic signs in a diagonally divided field forms the basic pattern. The pair as a unity communicates harmony, the diagonal division tension. In the version illustrated one half contains the motif of a stylized feline-cum-human head with typical divided eye and tearmarks. The other triangular space is filled with a step meander which stands for a bird's wing. Presumably the winged feline god, reduced to a concise formula, is depicted here as religious symbol elevated to the supernatural realm inexplicable to men.
South Coast, Tiahuanaco-Huari style, c. 600–900.
Diameter of bowl c. 18 cm.; detail of textile c. 38×30 cm.
Private collection

92 On the complete textile from which this detail comes, the staff-bearer, dissolved into cube-like forms, is repeated in alternating colours.
South Coast, Tiahuanaco-Huari style, c. 600–800.
Size of one figure 22×20 cm.
Private collection

93 Tapestry fragment with the diagonal double motif. Multi-coloured alpaca weft on cotton warp.
South Coast, Tiahuanaco-Huari style, c. 600–900.
12.5×31 cm.
Private collection

94 Tapestry fragment with a variation of the diagonal double motif. The pattern is formed by two highly stylized bird's wings facing each other, arranged regularly in pairs as an ornamental strip.
South Coast, Tiahuanaco-Huari style, c. 600–900.
Width of pattern strip 36 cm.
Private collection

95 Fragment of tapestry with the 'composite motif', in which four or eight abstract figurative elements are combined in rectangular fields in such a way that they produce a further picture when seen together.
South Coast, Tiahuanaco-Huari style, c. 700–900.
c. 21×12.5 cm.
Private collection

96 Detail of a man's poncho in tapestry technique with the composite motif.
South Coast, Tiahuanaco-Huari style, c. 700–900.
Size of one face of garment 99×108 cm.
Textile Museum, Washington, D.C.

97 Shirt with the diagonal double motif as seen in Pl. 94. The careful execution of this tapestry suggests that it was made in the highlands or by highland weavers who had moved to the coast.
South Coast, Tiahuanaco-Huari style, c. 600–800.
Size of one face of garment c. 100×120 cm.
David Bernstein Collection, New York

98 Fragment with a different kind of composite motif. Tapestry, alpaca on cotton warp.
South Coast, Tiahuanaco-Huari style, *c.* 700–900.
Height *c.* 25 cm.
Rietberg Museum, Zurich

99 Detail of a garment: squares with a red stripe pattern alternate with squares in which various highly stylized anthropomorphic creatures are depicted holding birds and staves. It is impossible to guess whether this tapestry depicts priests in procession, warriors breaking camp or tribal chieftains hunting, because there is as yet no clue in another medium (such as stone relief or painted ceramics) which might help in interpretation.
Tapestry, alpaca on cotton warp.
South Coast, Tiahuanaco-Huari style, *c.* 600–1000.
Size of one face of garment 105×110 cm.
Textile Museum, Washington, D.C.

100, 101 Double spout and bridge vessel and tapestry fragment.
South Coast, Tiahuanaco-Huari style, *c.* 600–900.
Height of vessel 14 cm.; textile 16.8×16 cm.
Private collection, Switzerland

102 Tapestry fragment with the dimly remembered motif of the staff-bearer. This is a work of which the weaver was no longer familiar with the classic pattern.
Probably Central or North Coast, Tiahuanaco-Huari style, *c.* 700–1000.
Height *c.* 8 cm.
Private collection, London

103 Textile fragment with chequer pattern. The upper ornamental strip is composed of mythical birds of prey in rectangular fields. The central theme is a geometric double-headed snake terminating in highly stylized feline heads seen in profile. The ground (plain weave/rep with concealed weft) consists of cotton yarn, while the weft threads with additional brocading threads are mostly of alpaca wool. In this kind of textile weavers were trying to imitate rep with concealed warp, i.e. genuine tapestry.
Central Coast (Pachacamac?), late Tiahuanaco-Huari style, *c.* 800–1000.
c. 35×40 cm.
Textile Museum, Washington, D.C.

104 Tapestry fragment with chequer pattern in which birds and other animals (possibly conjoined llamas) are depicted.
South or Central Coast, late Tiahuanaco-Huari style, *c.* 700–1000.
38×36 cm.
Private collection, Zurich

105 Part of large tapestry fragment, alpaca wool on cotton warp. The pattern consists of rows of human-cum-feline heads depicted in profile. The motifs on the headdress and the face painting are geometric and exhibit small variations. The arrangement in fields has led some scholars to speculate that it might be a system of writing or calendar signs.
Probably South Coast, Tiahuanaco-Huari style, *c.* 600–1000.
Detail *c.* 30×60 cm.
Brooklyn Museum, New York

106 Fragment showing a feline, far removed from the staff-bearer prototype. Alpaca wool brocade on plain weave cotton fabric.
Northern Central Coast, Huarmey, late Tiahuanaco-Huari style, *c.* 700–1000.
29.5×20 cm.
Private collection

107 Ornamental hem of a slit tapestry robe of alpaca wool with fabulous cat-like figures and geometric patterns.
Northern Central Coast, Huarmey, Tiahuanaco-Huari style, *c.* 600–900.
90×25 cm.
Private collection, New York

108 Detail of an ornamental band with mythical figures in cult attire. Cotton and alpaca weft on cotton warp.
Central Coast (?), late Tiahuanaco-Huari style, *c.* 800–1000.
Size of one figure *c.* 12.5×16.5 cm.
Textile Museum, Washington, D.C.

109 Cotton fabric decorated by tie-dyeing.
Southern Highlands, early Tiahuanaco culture, *c.* 200–800.
58.5×60.5 cm.
André Emmerich Gallery Inc., New York

110 Slit tapestry fragment depicting a human figure. Wool and cotton.
Central or North Coast, late Tiahuanaco-Huari style, *c.* 800–1000.
9×11.5 cm.
Private collection

111 Slit tapestry fragment depicting a human figure. Wool and cotton.
Central or North Coast, late Tiahuanaco-Huari style, *c.* 800–1000.
9.5×19 cm.
Edward H. Merrin Gallery, New York

112 Detail of a band ornamented with birds of prey. Rep with concealed warp; weft of wool, probably alpaca, on cotton warp.
South Coast (Ica?), late Tiahuanaco-Huari style, *c.* 800–1000.
Size of one figure *c.* 4.5×6.5 cm.
Private collection

113, 114 Two ornamental bands. Rep with concealed warp in the undecorated part, with slit tapestry, alpaca and cotton.
Northern Central Coast, late Tiahuanaco-Huari style, *c.* 800–1000.
6.15×20 cm.; 12×18 cm.
Private collection

115–117 Three headdresses in 'simili-velours' (imitation velvet) technique. As Harcourt explains, this usually consists of a network made with a single yarn using the Chinese or square knot. The special feature is the incorporation of an independent wool yarn along with the network yarn during knotting. The independent yarn, caught between two knots, forms loops which when cut form pile.

The method of fabrication and especially the shape of the four-cornered 'night-cap' came into fashion on the coast through the Huari culture in the Middle Horizon, whereas highlanders preferred a headdress with earflaps of the kind still worn by mountain Indians today (Pl. 8). The motifs in Pl. 117 are llamas

accompanied by young animals and, as the 'X-ray representation' shows, with an unborn offspring inside the body. The four-pointed pile-woven cap (Pl. 115) and the four-cornered 'hat' (Pl. 116) exhibit local variations of the staff-bearer motif.
South Coast, Tiahuanaco-Huari style, *c.* 600–900.
Height: 14.6 cm.; 12 cm.; 8 cm.
David Bernstein Collection, New York (115, 116); private collection (117)

118 Tassel depicting a god with a headdress consisting of a double-headed snake. Wool embroidery on a cotton core.
South or Central Coast, late Tiahuanaco-Huari style, *c.* 800–1000.
Total height *c.* 9 cm.
Private collection

119 Detail of a cotton openwork textile (cf. caption for Pl. 22) depicting highly stylized demon faces or Oculate Beings (?). These gauzes give much scope for abstraction and their transparency enhances the ethereal quality of the pattern. The textiles of the Late Intermediate period differ from their predecessors by their technical variety and wider range of subjects.
Central Coast, Chancay or Ancón, *c.* 1000–1400.
Detail *c.* 12×9 cm.
Private collection

120 Large fabric, probably part of a wall-hanging, showing a monkey-like creature in an aggressive or imploring attitude with its young. Brocade in dyed wool on plain weave cotton fabric with upper and lower borders in tapestry, the whole cloth the same width as a loom.
Central Coast, Chancay, *c.* 1000–1200.
111×55 cm.
Private collection

121 Tapestry pattern band with numerous motifs. Fabrics of this kind often formed part of the grave goods of weavers as an example of their skill or as a sampler, together with other implements of their craft. These 'notebooks' contain a large number of textile patterns in the smallest possible space (see p. 16 and Fig. 12).
Central Coast, Chancay, *c.* 1000–1400.
39×17 cm.
Private collection

122 Stirrup-spout vessel with a pattern of interlocking snakes.
North Coast, Moche culture, Early Intermediate Period, *c.* 100–600.
Height 18 cm.
Private collection, Switzerland

123 Detail of an interlocking snake pattern incised in adobe, from the pyramid of Licapa.
North Coast, Chicama valley, Early Intermediate Period, *c.* 300 BC–AD 300.

124 Openwork gauze ornamented with interlocking snakes.
The juxtaposition of this fabric with the much earlier vessel and adobe decorated with the same interlocking snake pattern shows clearly how Peruvian craftsmen clung to certain favourite motifs and shapes through the centuries, or, after periods in which other styles predominated, returned to old traditions and breathed new life into them.

Central Coast, Chancay, *c.* 1000–1400.
25×50 cm.
Private collection

125 A youth's garment with two felines as the main decoration; the border motif consists of interlocking birds. Supplementary brocading on rep weave (cp. notes on Pls. 20, 21), wool on cotton warp.
South Coast, Ica, *c.* 1000–1400.
40×37 cm.
CDO Collection

126 Demons and animals, and geometric patterns, brocaded on a plain weave cotton fabric.
Central Coast, Chancay, *c.* 1000–1400.
76×112 cm.
André Emmerich Gallery Inc., New York

127 Sea bird with outspread headdress, holding a fish creature in its long curved beak, framed by coloured stripes. Brocading on plain weave cotton fabric.
Central or South Coast, *c.* 1000–1400.
Motif 29×36.5 cm.
Private collection

128 Frogs or toads embroidered in alternately pink and yellow alpaca wool on brown plain weave cotton cloth.
Central or South Coast, *c.* 1000–1400.
14.5×13 cm.
Private collection

129 Small mother-of-pearl carving in the form of a frog or toad with inlaid eyes. Such carvings served, as did small metal platelets or shells, as applied ornaments for clothing.
Central or South Coast, *c.* 1000–1400.
Height *c.* 5 cm.
CDO Collection

130, 131 Cat-like creatures, and stylized deer with antlers, brocaded in pale yellow, ochre and pink on dark brown plain weave cotton.
Central Coast, Chancay, *c.* 1000–1400.
9×17 cm.; 13.5×9 cm.
Private collection

132 Cotton fabric brocaded with birds holding trophy heads in their beaks – a traditional pattern that survived for centuries.
Central Coast, Pachacamac, *c.* 1000–1400.
c. 30×40 cm.
CDO Collection

133 Brocaded fragment with sewn-on fringe. The main motif, in monochrome on a plain weave cotton fabric, is a very ancient type of bird motif (bird within a bird), whereas the multi-coloured wool border shows an interlocking bird motif.
North Coast, *c.* 1000–1400.
22×13 cm.
Private collection

134 Birds embroidered in alpaca yarn dyed in different colours on a plain weave cotton fabric.
Central Coast, *c.* 1000–1400.

24.5×11 cm.
Private collection

135 This coarsely woven cotton cloth betrays clumsy workmanship, yet in the effort at realism the 'artist' achieved a sensitive representation of a bird very similar to the great works of many 'naive' painters of the twentieth century. Dyed llama wool embroidery on an undyed cotton ground.
Central Coast, Chancay, c. 1000–1400 (or earlier).
16×25 cm.
Private collection

136, 137 Fragments with interlocking bird patterns produced by the use of stencils. That in Pl. 136 has dark brown painting on undyed cotton; that in Pl. 137, covering colours in yellow, salmon pink, turquoise and dark brown.
Central and North Coast, c. 1000–1400.
17.5×15 cm.; 13.5×13 cm.
Private collection

138 Fragment with realistically depicted sea birds alternating in diagonal stripes with interlocking snakes or fish. Painted in yellow, turquoise blue and several shades of brown on undyed cotton.
Central Coast (?), c. 1000–1400.
c. 35×50 cm.
Private collection

139 Front of a garment in slit tapestry. Alpaca wool on undyed cotton warp (brown and beige).
North Coast (?), Chimu (?), c. 1000–1400.
60×50 cm.
Private collection

140 Border with fringe. Slit tapestry with additional brocading threads, llama or alpaca wool.
North or Central Coast, c. 1000–1400.
Width of border c. 13 cm.
Private collection, Switzerland

141 Long cotton fabric, on which humming-birds (?) alternate with geometric ornaments.
Central Coast, c. 1300–1450.
c. 206–37 cm.
André Emmerich Gallery Inc., New York

142 Above: hem of a robe with ornamental fringes. Slit tapestry in alpaca wool with additional embroidery and applied elements.
Width of hem c. 15 cm.
Below: hem without visible seam between it and the fringe. The ornamental motifs are joined by a coarse-meshed netting. These openwork areas were deliberately introduced to form the pattern. Cotton and dyed alpaca wool.
Width of hem 28 cm.
North and Central Coast, Early Chimu and Chimu style, c. 1000–1400.
Private collection

143 Detail of a painted cotton fabric with a pattern consisting of diagonal stripes with interlocking birds separated by a zigzag band.

North or Central Coast, Chancay (?), c. 1000–1400.
c. 140×110 cm.
André Emmerich Gallery Inc., New York

144, 145 Relief decoration at Chanchan. Commercial contacts and the great military campaigns by the Chimu helped these patterns to spread throughout the North and Central Coasts. The individual motifs are 40–70 cm. high.
Chimu culture, c. 1200–1450.

146 Detail of the partially restored pyramid known as the Huaca del Dragón near Chanchan. Unlike the bird motifs found on the walls of the city, these mythological compositions are more closely connected with the conceptual world of the inhabitants of the North Coast. Pictorial records such as this scene and those shown on painted cloths (Pls. 151–153) are especially valuable in the absence of written sources.
Chimu culture, c. 1200–1450.

147 Double-cloth pattern band, showing motifs used to decorate ornamental borders on clothing, and accessories such as belts, headbands and coca bags. From top to bottom: interlocking bird motif; striped band in a different weave; strip with geometric motifs and a pattern in which a stylized bird is combined with an Oculate Being; bird motif resembling the adobe figures at Chanchan; stylized birds (humming birds?) and geometric patterns. Undyed and brown wool.
Central Coast, Chancay, c. 1000–1400.
28×11.5 cm.
Private collection

148 Bowl with polychrome geometric patterns.
South Coast, Ica style, c. 1000–1450.
Diameter 21.5 cm.
University Museum of Archaeology and Ethnology, Cambridge

149 Bowl with polychrome geometric and figurative patterns.
South Coast, Ica style, c. 1000–1450.
Height c. 12 cm.
Lindenmuseum, Stuttgart

150 Fragments of a painted cotton fabric depicting fishermen or warriors in boats on the sea.
North Coast (?), Chimu (?), c. 1000–1400.
48×28 cm.
Private collection

151 Painted cotton fabric, probably part of a wall-hanging, with a full-length human figure, probably a cult dancer, standing below a jagged snake. The sign like a starfish at the lower right may symbolize the moon or, more specifically, all the waxing and waning phases of that planet which, on the coast, was more honoured than the sun. Yellow, red and bluish grey on undyed cotton.
Northern Central Coast (Huarmey?), c. 1000–1400.
63×133 cm.
Museum für Völkerkunde, Munich

152 Painted cotton fragment with mythological representations. The figure is outlined in dark brown.
North Coast, Chimu, c. 1000–1250.
144×133 cm.
Museum für Völkerkunde, Munich

153 Painted fabric depicting a religious ceremony probably connected with the sacrifice of a captured warrior. Three friezes around this central field show cat-like beings, double-headed snakes and further prisoners. Yellow, brown and turquoise on undyed cotton. Junius Bird showed that this large cloth originally formed part of a vast wall-hanging 32.25 m. long, presumably cut up into twenty separate pieces when it was discovered; Bird reconstructed it from thirteen fragments that he tracked down in different museums and private collections.
Probably North Coast, Chimu (?), c. 1000–1250.
c. 185×175 cm.
Textile Museum, Washington, D.C.

154 Pattern sample of an interlocking bird motif, brocaded on a plain weave cotton fabric.
Central or North Coast, c. 1000–1400.
5.4×5.5 cm.
Private collection

155, 156 Two ornamental pieces. In each the central figure is flanked by birds holding a fish in their beaks. Slit tapestry of alpaca wool on cotton warp.
Central Coast, Chancay, c. 1000–1400.
31.2×30.8 cm., figure 21×20 cm.
Edward H. Merrin Gallery, New York

157 Decorative piece with fringed hems at both ends. The central part is arranged in rectangular fields in which human figures alternate with S-shaped motifs, perhaps representing the double-headed snake. Brocaded in shades of brown wool on plain weave undyed cotton.
Central part of the North Coast, c. 1000–1400.
39×27 cm.
CDO Collection

158 Slit tapestry showing three highly stylized figures with headdresses and raised hands, on a red ground.
South Coast, Ica valley, c. 1000–1400.
26×40 cm.
Private collection

159 Fragment of double-cloth in light beige and dark brown cotton. The motif, a hybrid, appears on the reverse in the opposite colour scheme.
North Coast (?), c. 1000–1450.
c.28×17 cm.; height of one motif c. 5 cm.
Private collection

160 Fragment of double-cloth in light beige and dark brown cotton with a bird motif formed into an ornament.
North Coast (?), c. 1000–1450.
11.8×8 cm.
Private collection

161 Detail of a fragment of slit tapestry depicting roe deer or red deer. The stylized antlers resemble the sickle-shaped headdress of the inhabitants of the North Coast.
North or Central Coast, c. 1000–1400.
Complete fragment c. 24×18 cm.
Edward H. Merrin Gallery, New York

162 Three ornamental tassels with anthropomorphic figures in slit tapestry, with fringed border.

Central Coast, Chancay, c. 1000–1400.
Height of figures c. 15 cm.
Edward H. Merrin Gallery, New York

163 Detail of a border with horizontally arranged human figures. Although the sickle-shaped headdress which these figures wear was characteristic of North Coast dress, especially for high dignitaries of the Moche culture (see Fig. 67), the sites where this particular kind of textile is known to have been found are on the Central Coast, e.g. at Pachacamac and Chancay. Slit tapestry with brocaded ornamental stripes.
North or Central Coast, Chancay or Chimu, c. 1000–1400.
Height of figure c. 5 cm.
L. J. Handler Collection, Vienna

164 Fragment of a man's garment in slit tapestry with stylized human figures and fish motifs. It is impossible to say whether the figures represent protective sea spirits or contemporary warrior chiefs.
North Coast, Chimu, c. 1100–1400.
74×80 cm.
Private collection, New York

165 Large shirt with a pattern of human figures with ropes round their necks and rows of zoomorphic creatures. Embroidery and 'appliqué' borders on loose plain weave ground with wool brocading.
North Coast, Pacatnamú, Chimu, c. 1000–1400.
Size of one face of garment 79×129 cm.
Odeon Gallerie, Munich

166 Slit tapestry fragment showing two hybrid creatures.
Central Coast, Chancay valley, c. 1300–1532.
Height of one motif 8.5 cm.
Private collection

167 Fabric with a chequer pattern in different shades of yellow, red and brown.
Central Coast, c. 1400–1532.
98×70 cm.
Private collection

168 Aryballoid jar of light-coloured clay with simple geometric pattern.
Southern Highlands, Inca culture, c. 1450–1532.
Height 28 cm.
Lindenmuseum, Stuttgart

169 Fragment of a man's garment with geometric patterned bands. Rep with concealed warp, wool on cotton warp, ornamental band in slit tapestry.
South Coast, c. 1400–1530.
Height c. 40 cm.
Textile Museum, Washington, D.C.

170 Fragment showing the 'morning star' motif alternating with a traditional bird pattern – a good example of the mixing of a purely coastal decorative motif with a specifically Inca pattern. Rep, wool on cotton warp, with supplementary brocading.
South Coast, c. 1300–1532.
c. 6×30 cm.
Private collection

171 Striped fabric in several techniques, wool and cotton.
South or Central Coast, *c.* 1300–1532.
c. 16×18 cm.
Private collection

172 Four fragments with geometric motifs.
Central and South Coast, *c.* 1300–1532.
From top to bottom, 7.5×10 cm.; 5×10 cm.; 3.5×10 cm.; right, 23×7 cm.
Private collection

173 Fragment with the 'leaf' motif. The term is not accurate, because this pattern was used to imitate sewn-on feathers, of the kind found on the ceremonial garb of high dignitaries (cf. Pls. 177, 178). Slit tapestry, wool on cotton.
Probably Central Coast, *c.* 1300–1532.
c. 10×8 cm.
Private collection

174 Poncho with geometric pattern. Tapestry in alpaca wool.
South Coast, Ica valley, *c.* 1400–1532.
170×98 cm.
David Bernstein Collection, New York

175 Large fabric, finished with fringes (rep) and horizontal rows containing bird motifs. Bird motifs also appear in the three lengthwise stripes, which alternate with fields of geometric ornament. Slit tapestry with supplementary brocading in parts, wool on cotton warp.
Central Coast, Chancay, *c.* 1400–1532.
195.6×96.5 cm.
André Emmerich Gallery Inc., New York

176 Ceremonial robe of a high dignitary. Slit tapestry/rep with concealed warp, alpaca wool on cotton warp, with 18-carat gold.
North Coast, Chimu-Inca period, *c.* 1400–1532.
103×84 cm.
Museo de Oro, Miguel Mujica Gallo Foundation, Lima

177 Feather poncho of a high dignitary. Both sides of this sumptuous garment are identical. In this technique the quill of each feather is bent back and attached to two cotton threads running across the base fabric of the same material.
South Coast, Pre-Inca or Early Inca style, *c.* 1300–1532.

Complete garment 152×84 cm.
David Bernstein Collection, New York

178 Detail of a featherwork fabric composed of large squares. Such textiles were at least 4–5 m. long; most were cut up by grave robbers so that they could be sold more profitably. This may not have been an item of clothing, but a wall-hanging used to adorn a temple or other religious building. For the technique and material see the note on Pl. 177.
South Coast (?), *c.* 1400–1532.
Detail *c.* 79×79 cm.
Private collection

179 Short shirt of extremely finely spun alpaca wool slit tapestry.
Central Coast, Huacho, Pre-Inca or Early Inca style,
c. 1000–1532.
Width 85 cm., total length 108 cm.
David Bernstein Collection, New York

180 Man's garment in slit tapestry of undyed brownish and whiteish cotton.
South Coast, Ica valley, Late Ica or Early Inca style,
c. 1400–1532.
Width 103 cm., total length 154 cm.
David Bernstein Collection, New York

181 Small shirt from the grave of a peasant. From the signs of use, we can tell that this modest garment in pale colours was worn during the owner's lifetime. Wool and cotton.
Central Coast, from the burial field of Chancay, *c.* 1400–1532.
Width 40 cm., total length 70 cm.
Private collection

182 Garment with chequerboard pattern and red triangular area surrounding the neck opening. Tapestry/rep with concealed warp, wool on cotton warp.
South Coast, Los Majuelos in the valley of the Rio Grande de Nazca, Inca style, *c.* 1450–1532.
Size of one face of garment 95×78 cm.
Museum für Völkerkunde, Munich

183 Headdress and ruff of featherwork, ornamented with sheet silver which also serves as a framework.
South Coast, Inca style, *c.* 1470–1532.
Private collection

Chronological Table

This table, read from the bottom upward, shows significant stages in the development of textiles, and the archaeological sites and regions where they first appear

Tapestry with wool warp and weft

Simple looping, as used in the threading of cross-knit loop stitch or the technique of simple looping through a base fabric

Continuous wool threads, slit tapestry and tapestry weaves with concealed warp, wool on cotton warp

Covering embroidery in wool on plain weave cotton fabric

Embroidery in coloured wool on plain weave cotton fabric

Painted cotton fabric

Cotton fabric with inset patterning (discontinuous weft)

'True' woven fabric in coarse plain weave cotton

Twined fabrics and nets made of plied cotton yarn

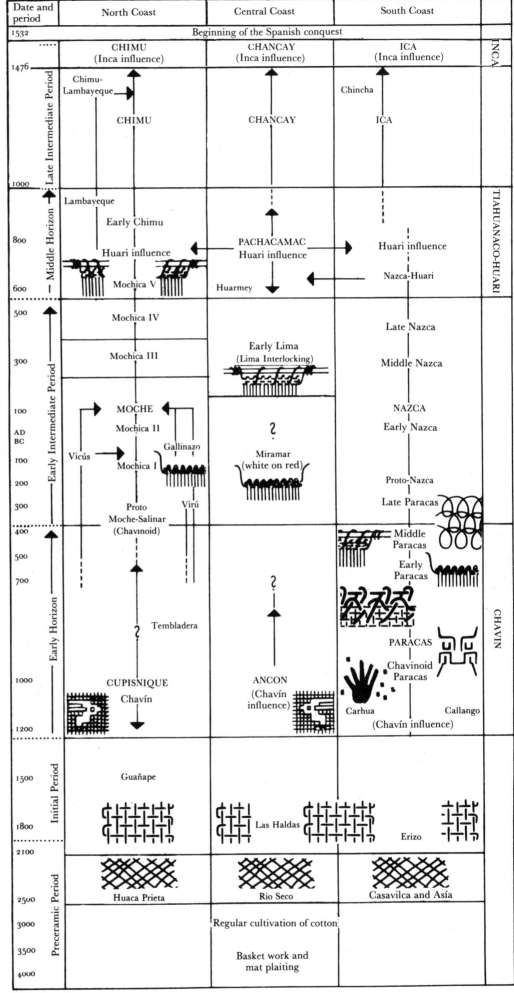

229

Textile techniques

1 *Simple looping as used in the threading of cross-knit loop stitch or the technique of simple looping through a base fabric*

2 *Avoidance of slits by interlocking round a common warp*

3 *Normal base structure for borders before brocading*

4 *Stem stitch embroidery; covering stitches which follow the structure of the fabric*

5 *Spiral netting as used for gauze*

6 *Openwork formation in combination with plain weave (after Harcourt)*

7 *Alternating float weave (with unevenly spaced warp)*

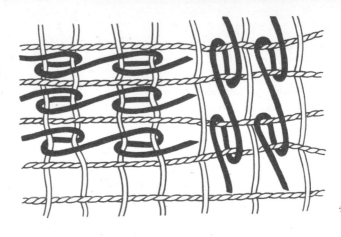

4

1

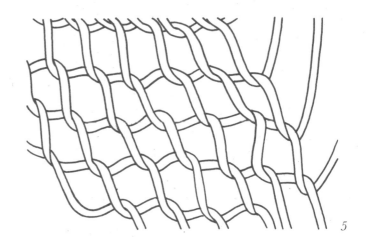

5

2

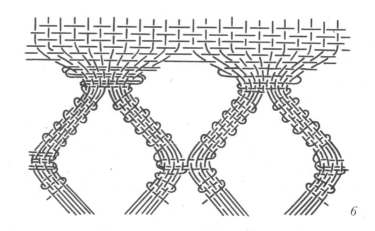

6

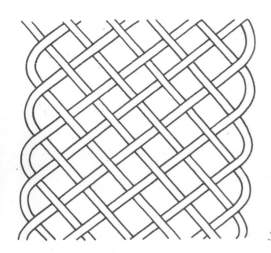

3

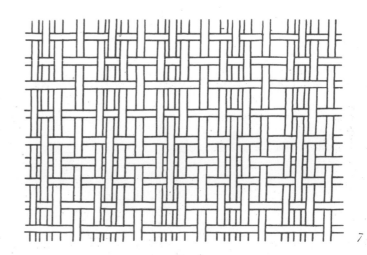

7

Select Bibliography

Articles in specialist periodicals are included when they have made an essential contribution to the study of Peruvian textiles.

ANTON, FERDINAND
Peru, Munich 1958
Altindianische Weisheit und Poesie, Leipzig, Munich and Vienna 1968
The Art of Ancient Peru, London 1972
Alt-Amerika und seine Kunst, Leipzig 1977
— with FREDERICK J. DOCKSTADER
'Das alte Amerika', in Thieme-Becker, *Enzyklopädie der Weltkunst*, Munich 1980

BAUDIN, LOUIS
A Socialist Empire: the Incas of Peru, Princeton 1961
BENNETT, WENDELL C. and BIRD, JUNIUS B.
Andean Culture History, New York 1949, rev. edn 1964
BENSON, ELIZABETH P. (ed.)
Dumbarton Oaks Conference on Chavín (with contributions by L. Guillermo, S. Izumi, D. W. Lathrap, L. G. Lumbreras, T. C. Patterson and J. H. Rowe), Dumbarton Oaks, Washington, D. C., 1971
BERLIN, NEUE BERLINER GALERIE
Präkolumbische Kunst aus Peru, exhibition catalogue, Altes Museum, Berlin 1977
BIRD, JUNIUS B.
'Technology and Art in Peruvian Textiles', in *Technique and Personality*, The Museum of Primitive Art, New York 1963, pp. 46–77
— and BELLINGER, LUISE
Paracas Fabrics and Nazca Needlework, Textile Museum, Washington, D. C., 1954
— and MAHLER, JOY
'America's Oldest Cotton Fabrics', in *American Fabrics*, no. 20, New York 1951–2, pp. 73–9

CARRIÓN CACHOT, REBECA
Paracas: Cultural Elements, Lima 1949
CONKLIN, WILLIAM J.
'Chavín Textiles and the Origins of Peruvian Weaving', in *Textile Museum Journal*, vol. 3, no. 2, Washington, D. C., 1971, pp. 13–19
'An Introduction to South American Archaeological Textiles with Emphasis on Materials and Techniques of Peruvian Tapestry', in Irene Emery, ed., *Roundtable on Museum Textiles, 1974 Proceedings, Archaeological Textiles*, Textile Museum, Washington, D. C., pp. 17–30
CRAWFORD, M. D. C.
'Peruvian Textiles', in *American Museum of Natural History, Anthropological Papers*, vol. XII, pt. 3, New York 1915, pp. 53–104
'Peruvian Fabrics', in *American Museum . . .*, vol. XII, pt. 4, New York 1916, pp. 105–91

DISSELHOFF, HANS DIETRICH
Alltag im alten Peru, 2nd edn, Munich 1981
DOCKSTADER, FREDERICK J.
Kunst in Amerika, vol. III, Stuttgart 1968
DONNAN, CHRISTOPHER B.
Moche Art of Peru, Los Angeles 1978
DRÄGER, LOTHAR
Das alte Peru, Leipzig 1964

EISLEB, DIETER
Altperuanische Kulturen I (with Renate Strelow, Christian Goedicke and Josef Riederer), Museum für Völkerkunde, Berlin 1975
Altperuanische Kulturen II: Nazca, Museum für Völkerkunde, Berlin 1977
Altperuanische Kulturen III: Tiahuanaco (with Christian Goedicke), Museum für Völkerkunde, Berlin 1980
EMERY, IRENE (ed.)
Roundtable on Museum Textiles, 1974 Proceedings, Archaeological Textiles, Textile Museum, Washington, D. C.
ENGEL, FREDERIC
Paracas, Cien Siglos de Cultura Peruana, Lima 1966
An Ancient World Preserved, New York 1976

GARCILASO DE LA VEGA EL INCA
Comentarios reales de los Incas, Lisbon 1609 and Cordova 1617, repr. Madrid 1960; English transl. by C. R. Markham, *The First Part of the Royal Commentaries of the Incas*, Hakluyt Society, London, vols. 41 (1869) and 45 (1871)

HARCOURT, RAOUL D'
Textiles of Ancient Peru and their Techniques, ed. G. G. Denny and C. M. Osborne, Seattle 1962

− and HARCOURT, M. D'
  Les tissus indiens du vieux Pérou, Paris 1924
HOLMES, WILLIAM H.
  'Textile Fabrics of Ancient Peru', in *Bureau of American Ethnology, Bulletin 7*, Washington, D.C. 1889

KANO, CHIAKI
  The Origins of the Chavín Culture, Dumbarton Oaks, Washington, D.C., 1979
KAUFFMANN DOIG, FREDERICO
  El Perú Arqueológico, Lima 1976
KING, MARY ELIZABETH
  'A Preliminary Study of a Shaped Textile from Peru', in *Textile Museum, Workshop Notes*, no. 13, Washington, D.C., 1956
  Ancient Peruvian Textiles from the Collection of the Textile Museum, Washington, D.C., The Museum of Primitive Art, New York 1965
  'Some New Paracas Textile Techniques from Ocucaje, Peru', in *Verhandlungen des XXXVIII Internationalen Amerikanisten-Kongresses*, Stuttgart and Munich, vol. 1, pp. 369–77
KRAUSE, FRITZ
  'Schleiergewebe aus Alt-Peru', in *Jahrbuch des Museums für Völkerkunde zu Leipzig*, vol. 8 (1918–21), Leipzig 1922, pp. 30–37

LAPINER, ALAN
  Pre-Columbian Art of South America, New York 1976
LARCO HOYLE, RAFAEL
  Peru, Geneva 1966
LIMA, MUSEO AMANO
  Diseños Precolombianos del Perú, 1981
LIMA, MUSEO NACIONAL DE ANTROPOLOGÍA Y ARQUEOLOGÍA
  Arte Precolombiano, 1: Arte textil y adornes
LUMBRERAS, LUIS G.
  La Arqueología como ciencia social, Lima 1974
  The Peoples and Cultures of Ancient Peru, Washington, D.C., 1974

MACNEISH, RICHARD S., *et al.*
  Readings from Scientific American: Early Man in America, San Francisco 1973
  The Central Peruvian Prehistoric Interaction Sphere (with Thomas C. Patterson and David L. Browman), Phillips Academy, Andover, Mass., 1975
MASON, J. ALDEN
  The Ancient Civilizations of Peru, rev. edn, Harmondsworth 1964
MEAD, CHARLES W.
  'Conventionalized Figures in Ancient Peruvian Art', in *American Museum of Natural History, Anthropological Papers*, vol. XII, pt 5, New York 1916, pp. 193–217
MEANS, PHILIP AINSWORTH
  'The Origin of Tapestry Technique in Pre-Spanish Peru', *Metropolitan Museum Studies*, vol. III, pt 1, December 1930, pp. 22–37
  A Study of Peruvian Textiles, Museum of Fine Arts, Boston, Mass., 1932
MONTELL, GÖSTA
  'Dress and Ornaments in Ancient Peru', *Archaeological and Historical Studies*, Gothenburg 1929
MOSELEY, MICHAEL EDWARD and BARRETT, LINDA K.
  'Change in Preceramic Twined Textiles from the Central Peruvian Coast', in *American Antiquity*, vol. 34, no. 2 (April), Salt Lake City 1969, pp. 162–65
  The Maritime Foundations of Andean Civilization, Menlo Park, Calif., 1975

MÜNZEL, MARK
  Herrscher und Untertanen, Indianer in Peru 1000 v. Chr. – Heute, exhibition catalogue, Museum für Völkerkunde, Frankfurt 1973–4

O'NEALE, LILA M.
  'A Peruvian Multicoloured Patchwork', in *American Anthropologist*, vol. 35, no. 1, Menasha, Wis. 1933, pp. 87–94
  'Peruvian "Needleknitting"', in *American Anthropologist*, n. s., vol. 36, 1934, pp. 405–30
  'Tejidos del periodo primitivo de Paracas', in *Revista del Museo Nacional*, vol. 1, no. 2, Lima 1932, pp. 60–80
  'Textiles of the Early Nazca Period', Archaeological Explorations in Peru, Part III, *Anthropology Memoirs*, Field Museum of Natural History, vol. II, no. 3, Chicago 1937, pp. 117–218 and 38 plates
  'Textile Periods in Ancient Peru: II, Paracas Cavernas and the Grand Necropolis', in *University of California Publications in American Archaeology and Ethnology*, vol. 39, no. 2, 1942, pp. 143–202
  'Weaving', in *Handbook of South American Indians*, vol. 5, Bureau of American Ethnology, Washington, D.C., 1949, pp. 97–138

PARSON, LEE A.
  Pre-Columbian America. The Art and Archeology of South, Central and Middle America, Milwaukee Public Museum 1974
PAUL, ANNE
  Paracas Textiles, Gothenburg 1979
POMA DE AYALA, FELIPE GUAMAN [HUAMAN]
  Nuevo corónica y buen gobierno (Codex péruvien illustré), ed. Richard Pietschmann, *Travaux et Mémoires*, vol. 23, Institut d'Ethnologie, Paris 1936
POSNANSKY, ARTHUR
  Tihuanacu, The Cradle of American Man, Hispanic Department, Columbia University, New York 1945

REISS, W. and STÜBEL, A.
  Das Totenfeld von Ancon in Peru, 3 vol., Berlin 1880–87
ROE, PETER
  A further Exploration of the Rowe Chavín Seriation and its Implications for North Central Chronology, Dumbarton Oaks, Washington, D.C., 1974
ROWE, ANN POLLARD
  'Interlocking Warp and Weft in the Nazca 2 Style', in *Textile Museum Journal*, vol. 3, no. 3, Washington, D.C., 1973, pp. 67–78
  Warp-Patterned Weaves of the Andes, Textile Museum, Washington, D.C., 1977
− with BENSON, E. P. and SCHAFFER, A.-L. (eds)
  The Junius B. Bird Pre-Columbian Textile Conference (19–20 May 1973), Textile Museum and Dumbarton Oaks, Washington, D.C., 1979
ROWE, JOHN HOWLAND
  'Inca Culture at the Time of the Spanish Conquest', in *Handbook of South American Indians*, vol. 2, Bureau of American Ethnology, Washington, D.C., 1946, pp. 183–330
  Chavín Art, An Inquiry into its Form and Meaning, The Museum of Primitive Art, New York 1962
− and MENZEL, D. (eds)
  Peruvian Archaeology: Selected Readings, Palo Alto, Calif., 1967

SAWYER, ALAN R.
'Paracas and Nazca Iconography', in S.K.Lathrap *et al.*, *Essays in Pre-Columbian Art and Archaeology*, Cambridge, Mass., 1961
'The Feline in Paracas Art', in E.P.Benson, *The Cult of the Feline, a Conference in Pre-Columbian Iconography*, Dumbarton Oaks, Washington, D.C., 1972, pp.91–115
Tiahuanaco Tapestry Design, The Museum of Primitive Art Studies, no. 3, Washington, D.C., 1963
Ancient Peruvian Ceramics. The Nathan Cummings Collection, The Metropolitan Museum of Art, New York 1966
Mastercraftsmen of Ancient Peru, New York 1968
Ancient Andean Arts in the Collections of the Krannert Art Museum, University of Illinois, Champaign–Urbana 1975

SCHMIDT, MAX
'Über altperuanische Gewebe mit szenenhaften Darstellungen', in *Baessler-Archiv*, vol.1, Leipzig and Berlin 1910
Kunst und Kultur in Peru, Berlin 1929

SCHULZE-THULIN, AXEL
Im Zeichen des Jaguars; Indianische Frühkulturen in Alt-Peru, Lindenmuseum, Stuttgart, Staatliches Museum für Völkerkunde, Stuttgart 1974

SELER, EDUARD
'Die buntbemalten Gefässe von Nazca im südlichen Peru und die Hauptelemente ihrer Verzierung', in *Gesammelte Abhandlungen zur Amerikanischen Sprach- und Altertumskunde*, vol. 4, Berlin 1923, pp.171–338

STINGL, MIROSLAV
Indianer vor Kolumbus, Leipzig, Jena and Berlin 1976
Auf den Spuren der ältesten Reiche Perus, Leipzig, Jena and Berlin 1981

STRONG, W.DUNCAN
'Paracas, Nazca and Tiahuanacoid Cultural Relationships in South Coastal Peru', *Memoirs of the Society for American Archaeology*, no. 13, Salt Lake City 1957

TELLO, JULIO C.
Prehistoric Peru, New York 1922
Antiguo Perú, primera época, Lima 1929
'Discovery of the Chavín Culture in Peru', in *American Antiquity*, vol. 9, Menasha, Wis., 1943, pp.135–60
Sobre el descubrimiento de la Cultura Chavín en el Perú, Lima 1944

UHLE, MAX
Kultur und Industrie Südamerikanischer Völker, Berlin 1890
Pachacamac, Philadelphia 1903
Wesen und Ordnung der altperuanischen Kulturen, Berlin 1958

VAN STAN, INA
'A Peruvian Ikat from Pachacamac', in *American Antiquity*, vol. 23, no. 2, Salt Lake City 1957, pp.150–159
'Textiles from Beneath the Temple of Pachacamac, Peru (A Part of the Uhle Collection of the University Museum, University of Pennsylvania)', *Museum Monographs*, Philadelphia 1967

WILLEY, GORDON R.
An Introduction to American Archaeology, vol.II, Englewood Cliffs 1971
(ed.) *Das alte Amerika*, Propyläen Kunstgeschichte, vol.18, Berlin 1974

The belt loom or back-strap loom, of the kind used by the Indians for three thousand years

1 Warp beam
2 Shed stick
3 Heddle rod
4 Sword
5 Bobbin with yarn wrapped round
6 Warp attachment
7 Belt or back strap
8 Warp threads
9 Weft threads

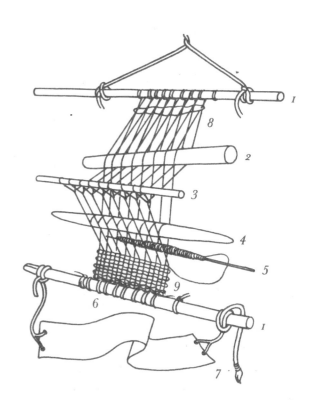

□ QUITO

Valdivia ▲ Chorrera

Tumbes ●

▲ Vicús

Amaz

Marañon

Huallaga

Ucayali

Lambayeque ●
Kuntur
Wasi ▲ ● Cajamarca
Jequetepeque
Pacasmayo ●
Chicama
Huaca Prieta ● ▲ Trujillo
Chanchán ▲
Moche ▲
Virú
Nepeña
Casma
Cerro Sechín ▲ ▲ Chavín de Huántar
Las Haldas ▲ ▲
Huarmey ● ▲ Recuay ▲ Kotosh
▲ Lauricocha

Marañon

Northern Highlands

Ucayali

Central Highlands

Paramonga ●
Mantaro
Chancay ●
Chuquitanta ▲ *Rimac*
(El Paraiso) □ LIMA ● Huancayo
Pachacamac ● ▲ Chilca
Asía ▲
Chincha ●
Pisco Ayacucho ● ▲ Machu Picchu
Paracas ▲ Huari ▲ ▲ Cuzco
Ica Nazca ▲ *Apurimac*
Nazca *Urabamba*

North Coast

Central Coast

South Coast

Southern Highlands

Pucara ▲

Lake Titicaca

Arequipa ● LA P

▲ □
Tiahuanaco

□ Capital cities

● Towns

▲ Archaeological sites

Index

Numbers in *italic* type refer to pages on which figures appear; numbers in **bold** type refer to plates and their captions.